King Pulp

The wild world of Quentin Tarantino

King

Pulp

The wild world of Quentin Tarantino

Paul A Woods

THUNDER'S
MOUTH
PRESS

First U.S. edition
First printing 1996

Published by
Thunder's Mouth Press
632 Broadway, 7th Floor
New York, NY 10012

First published in Great Britain in 1996
by Plexus Publishing Limited, London
This edition published by arrangement
with Plexus Publishing Limited

ISBN 1-56025-129-8

Cover design by Phil Smee
Book design by John Mitchell
Printed in Great Britain by Hillman Printers

Acknowledgements

The author would like to give special thanks to John Martin, who very kindly contributed the entire text of his interview entitled 'Tarantino Talks Trash' which originally appeared in *Giallo Pages #3,* most of which is reprinted in chapter 4, and thanks to John Williams for permitting use of quotes from his interview notes on Eddie Bunker. Articles and stories by the following also proved invaluable in doing research: Martin Amis, Ana Maria Bahiana, Peter Biskind, Henry Cabot Beck, Steve Chagollan, Godfrey Cheshire, John Clark, Jeremy Clarke, Jeff Dawson, Nigel Floyd, Graham Fuller, Dennis Hopper, Rod Lurie, Scott Macauley, Jim McLellan, Sean O'Hagan, Stephen Pizzello, James Ryan, Marc Shapiro, Tom Shone, Christine Spines, Quentin Tarantino, Amy Taubin, David Thomas and the BBC's *Omnibus.*

Film stills are courtesy of: BFI Stills, Posters and Designs; Channel 4; Ixtlan/New Regency/ Warner Bros; Live America Inc; Mainline Pictures; Miramax/Buena Vista International/ Disney; Morgan Creek/Warner Bros; Ronald Grant Archive; Rysher Entertainment/Savoy Pictures/Jim Sheldon. The publishers would particularly like to thank the BFI Stills, Posters and Design department for their cooperation and forbearance.

Contents

Tarantino on the set of Pulp Fiction.

Introduction

At the 1995 Motion Picture Academy Awards ceremony two young filmmakers took the podium to collect an Oscar for Best Original Screenplay.

Spurning the usual display of gratitude to everyone from executive producer to grandparents, the more upfront of the two – a wiry character with a lantern jaw – accepted the statuette with a subdued 'Thanks'. 'I think this is the only award I'm going to win here tonight,' he intimated, although nominated himself as Best Director, and his film, *Pulp Fiction*, as Best Motion Picture. 'I was trying to think, maybe I should say a whole lot of stuff, just blow it all, just tonight, just say everything.'

Behind him, his more subdued, long-haired co-writer shook his head. This was one speechmaker who, let off the leash, could ramble his way into the next millennium.

'But I'm not,' said Quentin Tarantino. And once more, 'thanks'. His co-writer, Roger Avary, had more time for the traditional sentimentality – 'I want to thank my beautiful wife, Gretchen' – but rounded off his acceptance with an unappreciated crack about having to leave the stage to take a piss.

The next day the film industry trade papers and the entertainment pages of the dailies were strangely reticent on the duo's surly nonchalance. In the normal run of things, they would have been taken to task for arrogance – Tarantino seemed excited enough to claim his prize, but he threw out the 'only award I'm going to win' line as if settling for second best – and their lack of awe. But their lack of protocol was quietly tolerated, the way swaggering rock stars are tolerated when they almost begrudgingly collect their Grammy awards. *The New York Times* reserved its only censure for awards host David Letterman, late-night talk-show darling and veteran of the entertainment industry, whom it felt had done a lacklustre job.

Why, then, so much acclaim, admiration and outright deference to a young moviemaker (to get the distinction straight from the start), and his writing partner? After all, they had created a gaudy, lowbrow entertainment with no socially redeeming value, no profound message, no earnest philosophy – in short, none of the virtues the self-righteous Hollywood establishment looks for in order to signify its own importance when it comes to dishing out the plaudits.

Despite the fact that *Pulp Fiction* didn't win six out of the seven Oscars it was nominated for, its very inclusion in the ceremonies seemed an antidote to that year's universal feelgood picture, *Forrest Gump*. *Pulp Fiction*, on the other hand, made anyone feel good who had an affection for the basic guns, gals an' guts sensibility of the lowest grindhouse movies and paperbacks. By refining that sensibility, its makers defined their own stylistic niche.

Tarantino's movies – which so far have resulted from his own tastes and obsessions, rather than any slick career moves – are the long-gestated children of the TV and cinema screen culture he was brought up on. Lack of critical snobbery allows him to regard any favoured 70s crime or kung fu flick with the same importance as the latest release from a revered arthouse director. For the last 30 years Quentin Tarantino has devoured and assimilated everything from that culture, knowing the importance of a cultural artefact like a movie lies in its visceral excitement and its visual iconography, rather than in the tackling of any worthy issues. The success of a Tarantino reminds Hollywood that it owes its very existence to creating thrills and entertainment. Significantly – but far from exclusively – Hollywood helped to shape the sensibility of a moviemaker who loves to celebrate the medium's cheap thrills and glamour, validating it with a knowing, referential context.

Add to that a love of popular culture in general – TV, comic books, rock 'n' roll, AM bubblegum music, fast food – and you have a talent that could only have come to flower in the early 1990s, when the post-boom babies, the pop-culture children, came of age. This book echoes its subject's celebration of lasting images from our supposedly disposable culture, and tells the story of his phenomenal success in the age he himself has helped to define.

CHAPTER 1

A geek is born

In 1963 the screaming mass media of the modern world had started to saturate the USA. Newspapers and TV force-fed a still reeling nation on endless photos, close-ups and blow-ups of its young president taking the fateful ride that blew away much of his brain, and brought him immortality; in the months to come, stills culled from the footage of the Texas motorcade by amateur cameraman Abe Zapruder would allow nearly every American family to share in their leader's assassination, in living rooms across the land.

At the movies, Alfred Hitchcock, the only truly major league director with one foot firmly ensconced in the camp of TV, then cinema's mortal enemy, had consolidated in *The Birds* the move he'd made with *Psycho* from suspense thrillers to terrifying modern gothic; audiences more familiar with his compellingly grim (and sometimes grimly funny) TV series – *Alfred Hitchcock Presents* – than his 50s suspense thrillers and 40s melodramas, queued for the thrill of our feathered friends turning blood crazy, pecking

Quentino Tarantino, playing one of the characters (Mr Brown) in his own Reservoir Dogs.

at the heads of hysterical children and swallowing a farmer's eyes (brought to the screen by the ingenuity of technicians from the Walt Disney Studios).

Even in a small southern nowheresville like Knoxville, Tennessee, the moonshine crooners of hillbilly songs were soon to be nonplussed by the emergence of a bunch of British kids calling themselves The Beatles, with their beatnik hairstyles and peculiar jangly kind of rock 'n' roll. Alien as their sound may have been, it wouldn't be long before local high school girls got themselves all het up in a screaming frenzy, the same as their cousins down on the East Coast or across the Atlantic, for this was a media-led invasion, starting right there in the corner of the living room, on *The Ed Sullivan Show*. This was the golden era of television – from here on, popular culture would always be inextricably bound to TV culture.

During this golden age of media saturation – on 27th March to be precise – a teenage mother in Knoxville – not much older than the kids who'd soon be screaming for The Beatles – gave birth to a baby son. Connie, the mother, was 16 years old, and realised, very quickly, that her marriage to Tony Tarantino, an unsuccessful musician, was a mistake. She soon decided to bring the boy up on her own. 'I never met my father,' the boy was able to claim in later life. 'My mom married him to get away from her family. Basically, they were bums. She ended up trading in one pair of bums for another bum.'

So much for the cold facts, now here's the legend: Connie was a half-Cherokee hillbilly, from a wild lineage of outlaw moonshiners, who sometimes left the baby with a semi-literate grandpappy who'd chew baccy while babysitting the child and the whiskey still. Sometimes, when the old man was off delivering his moonshine, the little boy would be left at the local drive-in, 'watching a dawn-till-dusk programme'.

With no favoured name to hand, Connie had named the boy after the character Quint, played by Burt Reynolds in the TV western series *Gunsmoke* – or Quentin, as she believed the unabbreviated version of the name to be.

Now in middle age, Connie is less than amused by the colourful legends surrounding her son's early upbringing: 'Most of what I read is untrue. Where are they getting these *L'il Abner* stories?' Rewind back to teenage motherhood, the southern locale, single parenthood – all of this is universally accepted as true, by everyone close to the resourceful young mother. What holds less Southern Gothic glamour, while paying greater testament to her personal strength, is that Connie didn't quit college, and graduated three years after the baby's birth.

Gunsmoke, US television's longest-running western, gave Quentin his first name, after Quint, a half-breed blacksmith played by Burt Reynolds. Tarantino's love affair with the mass media was sealed at this early point of his life, Gunsmoke *having been the top-rated series on American TV for the four years before the year of his birth.*

Moving west to Los Angeles, she married another musician, Curt Zastoupil. She also began a career in the healthcare industry, which she would pursue to executive level. Just a few years down the track, it would buy her and young Quentin a luxury home in an upper-middle-class suburb of Los Angeles.

For a time, the origin of Quentin Tarantino's seemingly Mark Twain-inspired early life was a mystery, as if a product of imaginative gremlins in the editorial works of entertainment mags. Then it was spotted by Jane Hamsher, an independent film producer in her early 30s and a former friend of Quentin's: 'He borrowed my family!' she laughed, incredulous.

In many ways Ms Hamsher seems to have had a much more bourgeois start to life than the young Tarantino: the offspring of a traditional two-parent family, her father educated at Harvard. But still, she can honestly claim that her mother is part-Cherokee, that her father's family hail from Nashville, Tennessee, and that, despite her father's middle-class orientation, they distilled and ran moonshine some generations back.

Her aspiring movie-maker friend had clearly spotted the magic in her own story; throwaway conversational details were picked up on as colourful fabrics to weave into his own personal mythology. Like any alert consumer of American movie culture, the young Tarantino could spot the importance of the newspaperman's maxim in one of John Ford's last great westerns, *The Man Who Shot Liberty Valance*: 'When you have to choose between the facts and the legend, print the legend.'

Young Quentin grew up in the South Bay, a sprawling area south of Los Angeles. Many years down the line, in the midst of recognition for his talents as an adult, his friends and colleagues could still detect traces of the little boy reared on the one-eyed monster. 'TV should never be ignored in Quentin's whole scheme of things,' lover and fellow movie-maker Allison Anders would say.

More poignantly, the actor Steve Buscemi would testify: 'When I saw *Pulp Fiction*, the little boy watching this big TV, being alone in the room, the TV being his friend – to me, that's Quentin.'

As a small child Quentin was Mom's constant companion, travelling with her wherever she went. In entertainment terms, this most often meant abandoning the small screen for the movies. In the very late 60s and early 70s Hollywood was experiencing a coming-to-terms with the freedom from the old Hays Production Code that governed from 1934. For a rare and short-lived period commercial cinema produced films that showed bloodily realistic violence and nude approximations of the sex act with little censorship, while still aiming their product at a discerning adult audience.

Connie saw no reason why Quentin's age should prevent her – or him – from enjoying the controversial new crop of Hollywood movies. The recently introduced ratings system meant that, theoretically at least, a child of any age could view any movie, as long as they were accompanied to the theatre by a responsible adult. (Most adult movies of the time were rated 'R', for restricted, the 'X' certificate – over-17s only – applying occasionally to erotic European movies, but mainly to the commercial underworld of porn.)

Abbott and Costello meet Frankenstein

TV provided the essential primary element of the young Tarantino's cinematic education, in the form of *Shock Theatre* reruns of the classic Universal horror movies of the 1930s and 40s. Like many a dream-absorbed child, he was in love with the monstrous archetype characters – the Frankenstein Monster, most powerfully played by the great Boris Karloff, the glamorously evil Count Dracula, immortally incarnated by Bela Lugosi, and Larry Talbot, the pathetic, reluctantly murderous Wolf Man, played by Lon Chaney Jr.

Abbott and Costello Meet Frankenstein was the absolute swansong of Universal's horror cycle, and was despised by movie historians and horror fans as a last-ditch sell-out of the famous fiends' dignity. The problem

Abbott and Costello Meet Frankenstein *(1948) – or, at least, are just about to.*

was Abbott and Costello themselves, for whom this movie was the first of several meetings with movie monsters; long regarded as 'the poor man's Laurel and Hardy', the comedy of these former vaudevillians/radio comedians was a faster-paced, largely verbal buffoonery that owed more to Bob Hope. The longer-standing, traditional horror fans hated them for what they'd done to their children of the night.

Young Quentin was not so stuffy: 'I remember the first movie I saw on television when I was, like, "Oh wow, you can do this in a movie?" was *Abbott and Costello Meet Frankenstein*. That was my favourite movie when I was five years old. The Abbott and Costello stuff was funny, but when they were out of the room and the monsters would come on, they'd kill people! And the big brain operation when they take out Costello's brain and put in Frankenstein's Monster's brain was scary. Then this nurse gets thrown through a window! She's dead! When's the last time you saw anybody in a comedy-horror film actually kill somebody? You don't see that. I took it in, seeing that movie. Then I saw *Abbott and Costello Meet the Mummy* [1955] and I remember thinking, these are the greatest movies ever made. You get a great comedy and a great horror movie – all together.'

'I don't think there's any such thing as "too funny", or that there's any such thing as "too hard". But I don't do it like *Abbott and Costello Meet Frankenstein*, where you're at the funny part, then you're at the scary part, then you're at the funny part again. To me, all my stuff is the funny part. If you were to tape an audience watching *Reservoir Dogs* and play it back, you'd swear you were listening to people watching a comedy.'

*Deliverance (1972), John Boorman's
study of city mores stripped away in the
face of natural aggression, was an
early influence.*

Making the most of this
cinematic liberalism, Connie took
Quentin from the age of six or
seven to movies such as *Carnal
Knowledge*, Mike Nichols' mildly
erotic study of that impenetrable
grown-up problem, 'relationships'. More importantly, she took him to see *The Wild
Bunch*, Sam Peckinpah's blood-spattered farewell to the days when no bullet could be
shown finding its mark, and *Deliverance*, John Boorman's intense, violent adventure
story pitting city slickers against nature, and the type of hillbillies who could make ex-
country girl Connie's blood run cold. Little Quentin was entranced.

As corporate life began to pay off for Connie, she was given season tickets for local
baseball and football teams, deciding to take along her son. 'I thought that would be a
great thing to take a boy to, but I couldn't get Quent to go to the games. He wanted to
go to the movies.'

The big screen and the cathode ray tube were the boy's salvation. It's easy to read
this as overstatement, but they were genuinely one of the few positive influences in what,
even as a young boy, Tarantino seems to have recognised as a negative social landscape:
'The Vietnam War and Watergate were a one-two punch that basically destroyed
Americans' faith in their own country,' he recalls, based on impressions received from his
family. 'The attitude I grew up with was that everything you've heard is lies. The
president is a monkey. I remember my parents saying, "Fucked-up pigs, they're jerks."'

This same attitude of distrust and dislocation, of unease in a dangerously deceptive
world, is what colours much of the atmosphere of the movies from Tarantino's favourite
cinema decade – the 1970s, his era of growing up. He was informed by the tough-but-
doomed individualism of Martin Scorsese, the funny/sick hopelessness infecting the gore
and splatter movies of George Romero and his disciples, and the desperate macho cries
of defiance that echoed out as the decade drew to an end and Hollywood entered its first
Vietnam cycle.

As for conventional education, school was not so hot. 'I was like the dumb kid who
couldn't keep up with the class,' he recalls. Spelling, arithmetic, even telling the time, all
posed problems for the boy. With his garrulous, hundred-word-a-minute adult
mannerisms already fully formed, the school officials considered him hyperactive and
wanted to 'balance' his personality with Ritalin. To her great credit, his mother refused
to allow the medication.

To the present day Quentin Tarantino has severe trouble with spelling, and when
talking excitedly, he mouths malapropisms, but all the manic, nervous energy that the

The Wild Bunch

Shot in and around the town of Parras in central Mexico, where Pancho Villa defeated the army of General Huerta in 1913, *The Wild Bunch* is rich both in bloody carnage and Peckinpah's themes of honour, loyalty, the hidden nobility of lawless men, and living outside of your time.

The basic story: after a robbery in Texas, where one of their number goes berserk and shoots hostages, an old-fashioned outlaw gang (this is 1914) escape across the border to Mexico, pursued by bounty hunters and a former compadre. General Mapache, a Mexican warlord fighting Villa, pays them to steal a consignment of rifles from the US army. The youngest of the bunch, a Mexican, pleads with leader Pike Bishop (William Holden) to be allowed to give one case of guns to the people of his village, to defend themselves against the army. Mapache finds out, and tortures the young Mex to death. The remaining four members of the gang return to avenge him. At the end of a bloody, protracted battle – in which the bunch commandeer a Gatling gun – all four are dead but so are Mapache and most of his 250-strong army.

The movie was the first of Peckinpah's 'ballets of bullets' – the epochal Western where every shot that hits home is observed, bloodily, painfully, in slow motion. As the director said: 'The outlaws of the West have always fascinated me. They were people who lived not only by violence, but for it. And the whole underside of our society has always been violence – it will be and still is.'

The grimly poetic fatalism was compounded by quietly unnerving images, such as the burning of ants and scorpions by a group of (mainly handicapped) kids. Production manager Phil Feldman says: 'The glares and looks of the bunch when they leave the whores [the only real parts for women in the movie] and they're getting together to go off and die, had a feeling. I'm not sure I could name any other guy but Sam who could have that detail in.'

The bloody impact of *The Wild Bunch* has survived its creator. (It has now been re-released in a completely restored print, after lobbying by Martin Scorsese and others.) It's not difficult to imagine the electrifying effect on little Quentin Tarantino – who first saw it in the very early 70s, in a double bill with the violently cathartic *Deliverance*. The classic theme of badmen trying to do the right thing, and dying bloodily for it, had never been so graphically portrayed. Its influence persists, not least in the doomed loyalties of *Reservoir Dogs*.

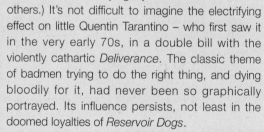

William Holden and Ernest Borgnine prepare for the end in The Wild Bunch *(1969). Tarantino saw the film at an early age, and it was to remain a seminal influence on him.*

school board disapproved of has been harnessed into creativity, and a mastery of modern speech no dusty text book education could impart.

Clearly, the young Tarantino had a nascent intelligence that wasn't going to translate into academic achievement. He scored in the 150s on school IQ tests, and was becoming a voracious reader. But still 'I fucking hated school. I was left back, so I was like, sixteen in ninth grade. I wouldn't even make the effort to just keep up with it, to do the little bit of work that I needed to do to get by. I wanted to be an actor. My mom didn't want me to quit school, because education was the bootstraps by which she pulled herself up out of a bad situation to a new life. I would act like I'd left for school and just go into my bathroom, which was downstairs, and bring a blanket and a pillow and spend those 90 minutes until she went to work just lying down in the bathroom. I would never really sleep because I could totally hear her walking around the house. It was like hearing a monster walking upstairs. Then I'd just fuck around the house. She would get real pissed. So we were arguing, and I said, "Well, guess what? I quit. Right now." "No, you're not going to quit." Then a couple of days later she came back and said something to the effect of, "Okay, Quentin, you want to quit. I'm going to let you quit. But you're going to have to get a job." And it was like, "Deal. Yeah, great. Yes! God, no more school!"

'I quit school when I was 15 or 16. I always wanted to be an actor, so that was the whole gameplan, to be an actor. When I quit school I studied with the actor James Best, who was the star of Sam Fuller's *Verboten* and *Shock Corridor*, and who at the time was the sheriff on the TV show, *Dukes of Hazzard*... Part of the thing Jimmy taught in his class was about camera technique, how to act for the camera. It wasn't about acting *per se*. 'Cos his whole idea was, "You're in Los Angeles, you're an actor, the way you're going to make a living is one or two or three lines on *Quincy*."'

Aged 17, Tarantino was working odd jobs to support himself while at acting class. He lived in the neighbourhood of Torrance, without a driving licence – which, in an auto-route city like LA, is pretty much like not having a licence to exist. 'I'd take three buses for three hours to get to it,' he remembers. 'The buses would stop running at a certain point at night. I'd whip out my sleeping bag and go to sleep at the school.'

'I studied acting for six years – for three years with the actor James Best, then for three years with Alan Garfield. That's been my only formal training. I never went to film school or anything like that. And then – I was right at the point, after studying acting for years and years, when it comes time to actually go out and start trying to get a career – I suddenly realised that I really wanted to be a filmmaker, because I really was very different from all the kids in my acting class. I was always focused on the movies. I knew a lot about them and that was always my love. They all wanted to work with Robert De Niro or Al Pacino – and I would have loved to work with them too – but what I really wanted was to work with the directors. I wanted to work with Francis Ford Coppola. I wanted to work with Brian De Palma, and I would have learned Italian to work with Dario Argento.'

'In the meantime, the only thing I could do was get a job at this video store because of my knowledge of movies. And it ended up being like my college, all right. It's not that

I learned so much about movies when I was there – they hired me because I was, you know, a movie geek – but it stopped me from having to work for a living, basically. I could just work at this place and talk about movies all day long and recommend movies all day long. And I got really comfortable. Too comfortable, as a matter of fact. It actually ruined me for ever having any real job because it just became like a big clubhouse.'

Video Archives was situated at the South Bay's Manhattan Beach. Tarantino was a customer before he worked there, and was encouraged to apply for a job by Roger Avary, a friend (two years younger than him) and member of Video Archives' staff. Over the five years that followed, the two would form a creative partnership, but initially the friendship was based on fierce movie buff competition.

In the 1994 BBC TV documentary, *Hollywood's Boy Wonder*, various co-workers got together to recount fond memories of their prodigious buddy. 'This is one of the few places where Quentin could come as a regular guy and get a job, and still be a star,' said one Gerry Martinez. 'Because he was like, "the star of the store".'

'We had a big-screen TV and we watched films all day long in the store. And I'd always put on stuff that I wasn't supposed to put on – you weren't supposed to put on stuff that had nudity or a lot of swear words, you know. But I was watching *Fingers* in the store. [An edgy 70s crime movie, with Harvey Keitel as a pianist who's also a habitual criminal.] And *Ms 45*, and wild stuff, Roger Corman women-in-prison movies. People would say, "What's this?" "Oh, that's Pam Grier."

'Also, because I knew a lot about films and everything, if I wanted to see something, I would buy it. I've been collecting videos since videos came out. And so my collection was able to completely enlarge.'

'A customer would come into the store and ask me about an obscure film,' says his then-employer Lance Lawson. 'I might be able to tell him what year it was directed, who directed it, maybe who the leads were. And Quentin would go on to tell you who the supporting cast was, who the director of photography was, who wrote the screenplay, and probably do a couple of scenes from the film, with the dialogue *verbatim*.'

Since childhood, Tarantino had been developing an admiration for the film criticism of Pauline Kael, and can quote many of her reviews almost word for word. It seems a little perverse, in that many of the genre movies – and certainly many of the exploitation movies – that he loves would fall beneath disdain for her. But, in teaching him that any movie, regardless of 'respectability', can be assessed, analysed, argued over, her influence has been profound.

'I kind of fancied myself the Pauline Kael of the store. People would come in and I would kind of hold court with them. Eventually – and this was great for the first three years, and a major drag the last two years – people would come in and just say, "What do I want to see today, Quentin?" And I'd walk them through it: "Well, this is *Straight Time*, it's with Dustin Hoffman, it's one of the greatest crime movies ever made," and so on.'

In the BBC documentary, Tarantino expounded on the geek philosophy, his *raison d'être*:

Rio Bravo (1959) is Tarantino's absolute No.1 favourite movie (amongst a plethora of other favourites) of all time – the film which makes or breaks relationships, depending on how a prospective girlfriend reacts to it. It epitomises the male bonding and camaraderie that he so admires in Hawks' movies, telling the story of how a sheriff (John Wayne – above) takes on defending the honour of his alcoholic deputy (Dean Martin). Tarantino actually goes so far as to credit director Howard Hawks with exerting a fatherly influence over him as a child, the young Tarantino learning what it means to be a man, to be honourable, and to have self-respect, from Hawks' celebrated ruggedly-American movies.

'The thing about film geeks is they have an intense love for film. Incredible love for film. Incredible passion. And they devote a lot of their time, they devote a lot of money. And they devote a lot of their life to the following of film. But they don't really have a lot to show for this devotion, except maybe a movie poster collection. The one thing they definitely do have to show for it, is they have an opinion. A highly developed opinion. But what you find out very quickly, here in Hollywood, is that this is a community where no-one trusts their own opinion. Everyone wants someone to tell them what is good, what to like, what not to like... Knowing more about movies than a lot of people in Hollywood isn't a big deal... Now – here I come. I'm a film geek. My opinion is everything – you can disagree with me, I don't care! I know I'm right, as far as I'm concerned, and I'll argue anybody down.'

The term 'geek' puts Tarantino, and the whole new wave of movie obsessives, on a different footing to their great-uncles, the 'movie brats' of the 1970s. Coppola, Scorsese, De Palma, Spielberg, all developed their fascination with cinema into some kind of career plan, studying the techniques, the theory and the history of movie-making as part of an academic education. Even where the movie-maker's knowledge of his medium was encyclopedic – as with Scorsese – and his love for the artform all-consuming, his development travelled along a linear path that took him from fan to student filmmaker to first-time feature or TV director. Similarly, his knowledge of film history would run in approved academic lines – from Griffith to Murnau, Ford to Kurosawa – with numerous little avenues of deviation where the nascent director could follow his own individual obsessions.

The geek, on the other hand, devours and assimilates everything that TV, video, the local multiplex and arthouse can offer him. His overview may be less structured, his opinions more eccentric – his relationship to cinema is purely personal, more often enhanced by movie magazines and books than by film-school training. The way in which his sensibilities developed allows little room for the respectable consensus view – *Citizen Kane* may be an okay movie, but it's not going to make his All-Time Top Ten.

Even the word 'geek' warns that his tastes may not earn what Tarantino calls 'the Good Housekeeping Seal of Approval'. Some equate the term with nerdishness, but its origins are a little more fearsome: the carnival geek was the bottom of the evolutionary ladder as far as American showpeople were concerned, lacking even the basic dignity of the freakshow performers. Basically a 'normal' guy in the throes of some kind of derangement, usually alcoholic, he'd roar at the crowds like the Wild Man of Borneo, and bite the heads from live chickens, all for the price of some straw to lie in and a bottle a day.

Gauche and hopeful, the 21-year-old Tarantino signed up with theatrical agent Cathryn James. The working relationship was long-lived and supportive, persisting right through the wilderness years, when fellow movie geeks – and movies themselves – were his only friends, but ended in acrimony.

'I hadn't done anything. So you, like, lied on your resumé. But since I was really knowledgeable about movies, I could put things down that either no one would have seen or that sounded good.'

As testimony to the breadth of his tastes, the young wannabe movie-maker's CV ranged from arthouse to hardcore splatter. What each genre had in common, apart from no appearances by Quentin Tarantino, was that they were Tarantino favourites – one favourite director, one favourite movie for each. 'I'd seen Godard's *King Lear*, and I was thinking, Oh, that's great, because that would look really impressive but no one will have ever fuckin' seen it. So my resume was like, *King Lear*, directed by Jean-Luc Godard, with Molly Ringwald, Woody Allen.' (Tarantino is now listed among the *King Lear* cast in Leonard Maltin's definitive guide to films on video.) However, genuine acting roles would not be generously forthcoming – though, poetically enough, he would eventually win the role of an Elvis impersonator in TV's old-broads-in-Florida comedy series, *The Golden Girls*.

At the opposite extreme to Godard, the young hopeful also said he had been a biker in *Dawn of the Dead*, a gory zombie film by George Romero that takes place in a future America where the recent dead stalk the streets. The film was also much admired by Roger Avary. If Tarantino really had been in the movie he would have been 15 at the end of shooting!

The video store guru took a tentative step towards becoming a writer by recreating scenes for his acting class that he remembered from the movies. 'Anything I couldn't remember, any holes, I'd fill in myself. I always knew that eventually I would be making films. It was really weird: there was never a doubt, but I still didn't really see it happening in the near future.'

It's clear it was his completist obsessions, rather than any affinity with the milieu of lawlessness, that later bred so many beautifully realised criminal characters – it took the man who knew the genre inside out to subvert it, to manouevre around all the established tricks and schticks. As for the naked aggression – in the dialogue and the sudden, brief bursts of action – that came from somewhere deeper within. The young Tarantino was far from being some AK47-toting gang member, but neither was he a spotty, timid film-buff nerd.

'Around junior high I decided that I wanted to be a tough guy. Did you ever hear that expression of, like, teachers saying about some kid who starts trouble, "Some day you're going to try that on the wrong guy"? Well, I just had this thing in my head: I wanted to be the wrong guy. I wanted to be the guy that the asshole started a fight with and wished he never did. I knew that the one who throws the first punch is probably going to win the fight, so if it looked like a fight was going to come up, I would just hit the kid right in the face and start taking him out right away. I became my own worst enemy, because then people would try to fuck with me, because I was one of the tough guys. I got it pretty much out of my system by the time I was 22.'

Not quite, according to best buddy Roger Avary, who claims there was still more than enough aggression left to go round at the time they worked in the store together: 'A customer came into Video Archives, where Quentin and I were both working. He came with a tape which was three months late. Quentin told the guy it was going to cost so much money in late fees. The guy said, "That's a lot of money. I'll just keep the tape," and started to walk out. Well, Quentin went after the guy. Quentin, with all his weight, went boom into the guy's chest and pushes him outside. He's pushing him, pushing him. And this guy was big. The thing about Quentin is, he's not afraid of stuff like that. He can take care of himself. He's lived in some hard neighbourhoods.'

Avary claims to have seen Tarantino involved in very many fights, most of which conformed to a set preliminary. Before any blows or kicks were exchanged, the film geek would make his opposite number wait a few seconds while he removed his earring, in case it was used to rip his earlobe. Somehow, the scenario seems to fit a Tarantino movie, but it's one he hasn't got around to using.

'I used to have a pretty bad temper,' Tarantino admits. 'It was really weird, though. I didn't get into fights at the drop of a hat. But, if ever someone threatened or challenged me physically, then I would go right at him. I could be really fuckin' mad, but I'd never cross that line. After all, words are words.'

As he drew toward his mid-20s, Tarantino recognised it was time to divert his energy into words and images. Into movie-making: 'I was 22 when I started at Video Archives. By the time I got to about 23, I decided to make a film. It was a film called *My Best Friend's Birthday*; it was a comedy, like a kind of Dean Martin and Jerry Lewis type of thing.'

The stylistic equivalent of so many student films, Tarantino's black and white trial run remains commercially unavailable. Technically limited and modest in its aims, it does, however, contain one notable sequence, which is not Jerry Lewis-style mugging and gurning so much as a tragicomic soliloquy for the TV generation. The speaker is Tarantino himself; his story, recounted to the character's friend, is told straight to camera:

'Out of the blue, I felt depressed for no reason whatsoever, just this dark cloud hanging over my head. I was gonna commit suicide. I was actually gonna commit suicide. I was gonna go up in the bathroom, fill the bathtub with hot water, and open my veins. I was actually gonna do it. Now for a three-year-old to be thinking like that, that's really depressing... You know what saved me?... It was *The Partridge Family*. *The Partridge Family* was coming on, I really wanted to see it, so I said, "Okay, I'll watch *The Partridge Family*, then I'll kill myself." Well I watched it, and it was a really funny episode, it was the one where Danny gets in trouble with the mob. And uh... I didn't feel like killing myself afterwards. It all kind of worked out.'

'We were shooting it for three years, and I thought it was like something really special,' admits Tarantino. 'It was kind of embarrassing when I looked at it again. Ultimately, I think making a movie is like the best film school there ever is. And so, it's like, I didn't know what I was doing at the beginning, now I know what I'm doing now. And I've had the experience, but now I'm not gonna do it like that any more.'

By the time of *My Best Friend's Birthday*'s completion, leaving dreams unfulfilled, Tarantino was already looking hard at his life: 'I was working at Video Archives for five years, and every six months I would have a Quentin Detest-fest. I would stay up all night and kind of go through all the things that were wrong with my life and give myself credit for nothing, like, You're a fuck-up, you

The Partridge Family *was a sitcom for children about a fatherless family who form a rock 'n roll band. The programme helped launch David Cassidy (top right) on a real career as a pop star. Tarantino's enduring obsession with the show was reflected in his first attempt at a feature –* My Best Friend's Birthday *– in which the Partridges save a character played by Tarantino himself from suicide.*

know? One day I had one of those Detest-fests, and it was, like, You have got to get the fuck out of the South Bay. You are judging your progress rate by your friends at the video store. And they're not doing anything as far as a career is concerned. You need to move to Hollywood. If you run with the fast crowd, you will run fast, even if you run last. The South Bay is far enough away from Hollywood to be a pain in the ass to go there. So you think twice, and if you think twice, you're dead. I had no money to do any of this. I was making less than $10,000 a year, and what you made in your tax refund was a good part of what you made that year. But I'd screwed around and hadn't done my tax work, and I had two years owed to me that I hadn't gotten. So after making this big decision that I was going to do all this, I got home at one in the afternoon, and there was a letter waiting for me. It was a cheque for $1,300, two years' worth of tax refunds that I had never taken advantage of. It showed up on the day that I decided to change my life. If I'd gotten it two years earlier, I would have pissed it away. Things like that, when they happen, it just makes you think. It was almost as if God was waiting for me to, like, get my shit together.'

Such an understated faith in the Almighty was not to rear its head again until the conversion of Jules the hitman, in *Pulp Fiction*. Till then, God, or whoever's in the driving seat, gave Tarantino a few false starts along the road, including a short stint working for a video distribution company and as an assistant on a Dolph Lundgren video, clearing dogshit out of a carpark so Lundgren wouldn't get his trainers dirty. Still, to strain a metaphor further, Tarantino was about to enter a higher gear and hit the open road.

'I wrote *True Romance*. I wrote it to be done for like a million/a million-three. For three years – at least for two years straight – while I was trying to get *True Romance* going, it was two weeks away. "In two weeks, we'll have the deal, we'll have the money, away we go." After a certain point, I said "Okay, this isn't going to happen. The reason it isn't going to happen is because I tried to get too much money when I haven't done anything."'

According to his agent, Cathryn James, and others – particularly collaborator Roger Avary – *True Romance* came into being through a more tortuous and interesting route. They concur that finance was the big stumbling block, as Tarantino was set on making the movie his own directorial debut rather than selling it on. Its origin, however, was in a script that Avary showed his friend and movie geek rival in 1987. Entitled *Open Road*, it was written two years before, when Avary was just 19. Tarantino was struck by the concept of the ultimate road movie, and suggested turning the two characters high-tailing it cross country into a couple of star-crossed lovers. He became Avary's collaborator on the script, developing the elements that excited him and adding the lovers on the run, Clarence and Alabama. When Tarantino took the script to another writer friend, Craig Hamann (his collaborator on *My Best Friend's Birthday*), for typing and editorial work, it weighed in at just under a hefty 500 pages. The concept began to split in two, the Clarence and Alabama element becoming *True Romance* and their more fiercely homicidal counterparts becoming Mickey and Mallory in *Natural Born Killers*.

Tarantino and Avary (with the former taking the lead as the main creative force) initially planned to produce and direct *True Romance* themselves, honing their script to a fine point over many months of late night redrafts and conversations. Using the customer database at Video Archives, they hoped to find enough wealthy business-people to buy shares in their project. Eventually, they did find one person with enough faith in them – British-born Hollywood business manager Stanley Margolis, who stuck with the project for the three years it took to sell and go into pre-production. By then, however, Tarantino had given up hope of directing it himself.

"So then I wrote *Natural Born Killers*. The whole idea was like, okay, I've written *Natural Born Killers*, and I'm going to get half a million dollars. Now, a year and a half – not quite two years – but a year and a half passes. And I'm a little further along than I was with *True Romance*, but we're not gonna be shooting film any time shortly. I finally said, "Look, nobody is going to give me money to make a movie, that isn't going to happen. Why would they?"

By this time, Tarantino had become equally tired of trying to get *Natural Born Killers* off the ground with himself as director as he was with *True Romance*, and passed the project to his intended producing partner of the time, Rand Vossler. By a convoluted route, Vossler would eventually recruit Hollywood's premier professional rebel, Oliver Stone, to direct.

'And by this time, it looked like *True Romance* was gonna sell. And so I was gonna have like Writers' Guild Minimum, which is what I was paid for the film. And it looked like I was gonna have $30,000... I hadn't worked at Video Archives for a couple of years, and for the last year and a half before I did *Dogs* I was like making a living as a writer, not a great living, but I wasn't having to work a day job. That was kind of cool, actually. In some ways I felt more excitement about not having to work a day job and being able to make a living as a writer than I felt when I realised I was going to direct *Dogs*, because from what I was doing to directing *Dogs* was a big-medium step, the biggest medium step you could make, but being able to make a living as a writer from working behind a counter – that's a huge step, that's like "Wow, I can like write now? I don't have to like go to work?"'

But going to work was exactly what was required now by the diktat of his dream; it was time for Tarantino, and eight edgy, desperate men to go to work.

CHAPTER 2

Reservoir dogs –
'Let's go to work'

Tarantino's new script evolved in three and a half weeks in the latter part of 1990, immortalised in felt tip pen in a single notebook. ('You can't write poetry on a computer,' he claims, but as he can't type, that's academic.) Frustrated by the failed materialisation of backing for the first projects he intended to direct (*True Romance* and *Natural Born Killers*), he expanded on an idea for homage to the pulp paperbacks and 'B' movies of the 30s, 40s, and 50s.

'And so I decided – I'm gonna write a film to do for thirty thousand – twelve days, $30,000 [from the sale of *True Romance*], 16mm, black & white, you know, starring some friends, and I will have a movie made and finished. By this time, I had met Lawrence, and Lawrence was a real godsend.'

Lawrence Bender was another young Californian hopeful, trying to find that all-important independent project to break his way into the movie business. (For details of

Harvey Keitel leads the gang in a publicity still taken during the shooting of the opening credits.

Harvey Keitel

Wiry, intense method actor with a piercing dark stare. One of the last prominent graduates of Lee Strasberg's Actors Studio in Manhattan, alongside friend and one-time co-star Robert De Niro. Keitel's self-contained but volcanic presence may owe something to his experience of 'real life'.

Charlie (Harvey Keitel) has just about had a bellyful of Johnny Boy (Robert De Niro), in a typically confrontational scene from Martin Scorsese's Mean Streets *(1973).*

Born in 1939; joined the Marines at age 17; posted direct to Beirut; left the service in his mid-20s; qualified as court reporter on his way to studying as an actor. First made an impact in Martin Scorsese's *Mean Streets* (1973), as Charlie, an angst-ridden debt collector from New York's Little Italy. Filling in with the obligatory episode of *Kojak*, Keitel teamed up again with De Niro in Scorsese's next masterpiece, *Taxi Driver* (1976); he is almost unrecognisable as the secondary character 'Sport', a junkie pimp with a fedora and shoulder-length black hair. In 1976 Keitel travelled to the Philippines, for the role of Captain Willard in Francis Coppola's *Apocalypse Now*. Coppola's arduous military-style regime irked him and he left to be replaced by Martin Sheen. After *The Duellists* (1977) Keitel would mostly eke out his career in a variety of unsung roles, until the role of a pugnacious Judas in Scorsese's controversial *The Last Temptation of Christ* (1988). At the turn of the 90s, an opportune series of roles was about to turn it all around: from the lead in the Poe-inspired horror movie *Two Evil Eyes* (1990), for Dario Argento, to the standard parts of policeman in *Thelma and Louise* (1991) and hoodlum in *Bugsy* (1992), then Tarantino's *Reservoir Dogs* (1992), and *Bad Lieutenant* (1992), Abel Ferrara's bleak account of a cop falling apart.

With *Dogs* and *Lieutenant* almost simultaneously to his credit, Keitel finally arrived in the style he had been threatening to since the mid-70s. A plethora of roles followed, some familiar – policemen in *Rising Sun* (1993), Michael Crichton's crime allegory about Japan overshadowing the West, and *The Young Americans* (1993), a British crime thriller – and some more quirky: Jane Campion's *The Piano* (1993), a story of love and obsession in New Zealand. In Abel Ferrara's *Dangerous Game* (aka *Snake Eyes*, 1993), he was an edgy, coked-up film director playing manipulation games with his female lead (Madonna) and in *Pulp Fiction* he was reunited with Tarantino.

his career, see chapter 7.) 'We were both very broke at the time,' he remembers. 'You know, he didn't have a car, so he couldn't drive over to my place. I didn't have money, so I wasn't paying for xeroxes. So I came over his place and I read the script. And obviously I flipped over it, it was an extraordinary piece of writing. And I said, "Look, you gotta give me some time. I think I can raise some real money for this movie."'

'No, no, no, no, no,' came Tarantino's reflexive reaction, 'I've heard that so much. Five years I've heard that, alright. I've tried to deal my way in for five years, and it was no sale.'

Compromise was reached, but with very little give on the writer's side. 'So he ended up giving me two months,' says Bender, 'which as I'm sure any sane person knows, that's insane. It's really an undoable thing, especially [for] two people who nobody knows about.'

And the written masterwork itself? 'It's a simple fact that I get a kick out of heist pictures,' explains Tarantino, 'so I thought I'd write one. I'd had the idea in my head about a film that doesn't take place during the robbery, but in the rendezvous afterwards. When I worked at the video store we had this one shelf that was like a revolving film festival and every week I would change it – David Carradine week or Nicholas Ray week or swashbuckler movies. And one time I had heist films, like *Rififi* and *Topkapi* and *The Thomas Crown Affair*. I started taking them home and it was in the context of seeing a heist movie every night that I put my head round what a neat genre that would be to redo.' Tarantino also came up with a title; it made little coherent sense but reeked of grimily poetic violence – *Reservoir Dogs*.

Mr White (Harvey Keitel) and Mr Orange (Tim Roth) at the armed robbery, from a publicity still for the film's German release.

For financial reasons most of the action was confined to the narrow parameters of a warehouse, where a gang of thieves liaise after a disastrous robbery. Tarantino's potential backers were telling him, 'This isn't a movie, this is a play,' but the wanna-be director's confidence never faltered. If he had to have his 'dogs' fighting and cursing it out in such a confined space, he was determined to turn every last square inch into cinematic spectacle.

Friends and supporters, including collaborator Roger Avary, were convinced this was the most polished, self-contained project Quentin had come up with so far. All the same, finance was going to be as grand a pain in the ass as ever; Tarantino was now prepared to shoot in 16mm on the laughable budget of $30,000. Then salvation came, in the granite-faced form of Harvey Keitel.

'Harvey had been my favourite actor since I was 16 years old,' testifies Tarantino. 'I'd seen him in *Mean Streets* and *Taxi Driver* and stuff. I didn't write the part for Harvey because I thought it'd probably be, you know, my Uncle Pete.'

In a quirk of smiling fate that's almost like the movies, Uncle Pete's chances of screen tough-guy immortality were cruelly reduced. Lawrence Bender happened to show the script to his acting class tutor, who just happened, in turn, to show it to his wife, a friend of Harvey Keitel.

'Keitel just called us up three days later and said, "Look, consider me in. Not only do I want to do it, I want to be one of the producers. I want to help it get made."'

'All of a sudden,' says Tarantino, 'we weren't just a couple of kids any more, with a script, just like everyone else had. We actually had Harvey Keitel. And then Monte Hellman came aboard [see chapter 4] – to just kind of act as godfather. He had done a film for the company Live Entertainment, so he got the script to Richard Gladstein.'

It was Live Entertainment director Gladstein who effectively made possible the scriptwriter's big ambition. The film would be credited as 'A Live Entertainment Production' as they effectively raised the budget. 'I made the assumption that whoever had written this must be an articulate, intelligent person,' says Gladstein. 'So, if he wrote this in the manner in which he wrote it, you'd have to give him the shot to direct it.' Cinderella was going to the ball at last.

Lawrence Bender noted Tarantino's obsessive attention to detail, meticulously planning every scene long before the cameras started rolling: 'Quentin shot-listed the production, from beginning to end, before we got into full pre-production. Then we cast the movie. And he was really nervous right before casting. But after the first person came into the room, he realised there was nothing to be nervous about. Then after all that, he went up to Sundance and directed a couple of scenes.'

The Sundance Institute was founded by Robert Redford, named after his nice-guy outlaw character in *Butch Cassidy and the Sundance Kid*. Situated in the snowy mountains of Utah, it exists to give first-time hopefuls in the movie business a chance to meet with professional filmmakers and writers, to showcase their formative projects in return for advice and inspiration.

Tarantino had very definite ideas about how he intended to use the Sundance facilities: 'I wanted to experiment on my first scene with long takes – I didn't want to do coverage, I wanted to just string a lot of long takes together and see how it worked. This was the first time since I'd got a little bit of the sense of what I was doing that I'd had a camera in my hand.'

The scenes rehearsed from *Reservoir Dogs* were those where Mr White, Keitel's character, sparks off of Mr Pink, with whom he's holed up in the warehouse rendezvous. For the trial run, Mr Pink was played by Steve Buscemi, the actor who would take the role in the movie, while Tarantino filled in the part of White.

All the rehearsals shot at Sundance are shown to a panel of filmmakers who give their initial responses and (supposedly) positive criticism. One of the directors first exposed to Tarantino's work in gestation was Terry Gilliam, former *Monty Python* animator and director of the fantasy epics *Brazil*, *Jabberwocky* and *The Fisher King*.

'Now Quentin was overlapping, this is what's kind of strange,' says Gilliam. 'He had the experience of two groups of professionals. And the previous group – whose names I won't reveal – had really been pretty rough on him, I think.'

'Really major league rough,' confirms Tarantino. 'They were saying, "Yeah, but these long takes, oh my God...", da-da-da-da-da, and like, "I didn't like that big wide shot." I did some big wide shot where it's supposed to double for the warehouse, where the camera's on the floor. And I liked it, I thought it worked really good, but, "I'm just seeing too much floor." Then I had this big shot in this mirror – "Uuuh" – they didn't like that, they didn't like anything. Anyway, that group leaves. And the next group comes in.'

The next group included, besides Gilliam, the German maverick Volker Schlondorff, director of the grotesque classic *The Tin Drum*. 'And our group loved Quentin,' says Gilliam, 'because here was a man with such incredible enthusiasm and this outrageous script, amazing energy, great dialogue, and just the sheer audacity of what he was doing. This is where the Sundance Institute was very useful, I think, as he went with all this energy and all these ideas, and this big chance to show everything he could do; and he did everything in these short scenes, he did it all, there were camera angles everywhere, the camera wouldn't stay still, it was up people's noses, down their throats, it was – wooh! – and you couldn't see anything. And I think that was a really useful thing for him to get out of his system.'

'Someone had a talk with him and said you're just gonna have to slow down,' says Steve Buscemi, laughing. 'But he had a lot of energy, a lot of enthusiasm at Sundance, and he had it on set too. I think he was able to hone his ideas more and he had more focus when we were actually shooting.'

'We had a two-week rehearsal period when we talked about a lot of things. It was one of the best rehearsal periods I've ever gone through. It was very thorough and we really explored every aspect of the script. We even rehearsed scenes that weren't written. We just made up different situations that these characters might be in: little improvisations... Eddie Bunker, who plays Mr Blue, was a real-life thief. So he was our unofficial technical adviser.'

Reservoir Dogs: Mr White (Harvey Keitel) and Mr Pink (Steve Buscemi) have a difference of opinion over what do about the injured Mr Orange.

Largely thanks to the intervention of Harvey Keitel, the movie had raised a still-modest but workable budget of $1.5 million. 'The thing was, we weren't fully financed when we started casting,' says Tarantino. 'We said, "Look, if we just wait around nothing's gonna happen." We were based in LA, but Harvey said, "We really owe it to ourselves to get a shot at the New York actors," and he bought our plane tickets, put us up in a hotel and set aside the weekend for a casting director friend of his to see actors in New York.' The trip added Steve Buscemi to the cast list.

'He had these eight different styles of acting, these different personalities to contend with, all very dynamic men,' says Keitel, breaking his usual laconic reserve. 'And Quentin won their confidence and trust from Day One.'

'All of the characters looked like they were going to be fun to play,' recalls Buscemi. 'They weren't simple, they were all complex. Half the time you were rooting for them, half the time you didn't like them, but they were always interesting.'

Pre-credits: six identically-dressed men – black suit, white shirt, black tie – are talking bullshit in an LA coffee house with a burly old man and his 30-something son. They argue about the meaning of a Madonna song. The old man insists they pay up and leave.

Title credits roll. All eight walk down the street in slow motion to the accompaniment of a 70s pop song, those in black donning shades. (Cinematographer Andrzej Sekula: 'We wanted to go for a more poetic movement. We wanted to give these gangsters a kind of unnatural slowness.') We glimpse a gun under one of their jackets.

Opens to black screen, screaming chaos on soundtrack. The picture focuses, we see two of the men inside a car, the younger man squirming on the back seat with a bullet in his gut, bleeding profusely. The older man tries to tell him he isn't going to die. He drives to a warehouse where they have arranged to meet someone called Joe, promising to call a doctor as soon as they arrive. The young man pleads to be left at a hospital, but it's no deal.

At the warehouse, they meet another gang member, an excitable young guy with a beard. He refers to the wounded young man – lying blacked out on a ramp – as 'Orange', and expresses his conviction that they were 'set up'. He and the older man – who he refers to as 'Mr White', insisting they continue to keep their names secret – recap on preceding events. They have been party to a robbery that went disastrously wrong, with one of their number – 'Mr Blonde' – shooting bystanders when a security alarm went off. In the first of many flashbacks we see how the bearded guy escaped by hijacking a woman's car and shooting a cop. Back at the warehouse the Beard reveals he has the diamonds – the object of the robbery – and suggests they cut the takings and run, as there's a 'rat in the house'. White reveals he was recently party to a robbery where one of the number turned out to be an undercover cop. The young guy insists they can trust nobody, not even each other. Flashback to White talking to Joe, who wants White in on the robbery of a diamond wholesaler, a 'five-man job'.

The Beard insists they escape, but White won't desert Orange. When told they should leave him at a hospital, he reveals he told the wounded kid his first name and where he came from. The Beard goes apeshit and White lays into him; they train gun sights on each other, point blank. Watching behind them is a tall dark-haired guy revealed as Mr Blonde. White tells him the score and suggests (having changed his mind) that they all get out of there. Blonde insists no-one is going anywhere. White loops the loop, blaming him for the disaster at the diamond wholesaler's. The Beard demands they stop acting 'like a bunch of niggers' and root out the traitor. (Blonde's psychosis convinces him he's no undercover.) Blonde directs them to his car, insisting they wait for 'Nice Guy Eddie'. In the trunk of his car, bound and gagged, is a uniformed cop.

Flashback: Blonde is at Joe's office. He is revealed as 'Toothpick Vic' Vega, fresh out of jail and a personal friend of Joe's. Joe is beholden to him. Vic says he's having trouble living under restrictions imposed by his parole officer. Eddie arrives, who is Joe's son; Vic and Eddie lay the obscenities on thick and 'piss fart around' in the manner of macho old friends. Joe insists they get down to business; they offer Vic a phoney docker's job (with real pay), and the chance to pull a heist.

'Real time': Eddie is in his car, trying to contact his Dad on the mobile phone. He leaves news that he doesn't know 'Who's dead, who's alive, who's caught, who's not…'.

Warehouse: Eddie arrives, White demands help for Orange, the Beard insists they were set up; Eddie is angry at them all for fucking up. He's told that Mr Brown is dead while Mr Blue's fate is unknown. Meanwhile, the uniformed cop is trussed up and has the hell beaten out of him. Eddie, White and the Beard go out to move their tell-tale cars from the front of the warehouse. Vic addresses the cop, who pleads total ignorance; Vic says it doesn't matter, as he's going to torture and kill him for fun anyway. He takes a straight razor from his boot and goes into a macabre song and dance routine to the radio accompaniment of 'Stuck in the Middle with You', cutting through the cop's ear and dousing him with gasoline. Vic is suddenly cut down in a hail of bullets. The camera pans back to reveal the blood-soaked Orange, returned to consciousness. He exposes himself to the traumatised cop as an undercover named Freddy Newendyke. He's been working to set up Joe Cabot; neither of them has any choice but to sit tight and wait for help.

Flashback: Freddy is seen crowing to a black fellow undercover that he's managed to infiltrate Cabot's operation. He gives his partner the lowdown on Mr White, who they identify from his baseball loyalties as coming from Wisconsin. He tells of his fake criminal credentials, and the help he received from a stoolie named Long Beach Mike, who his partner tells him to disregard. The black cop coaches him on a bogus story of involvement in the marijuana trade; the scene shifts and he's telling the story to Joe, Eddie and White in a club. His story of travelling by train to make connection with a buyer, and stumbling in on a washroom full of bragging cops, appears on screen as if 'true'.

Still in flashback:Eddie phones Freddy to tell him, 'It's showtime.' When they arrive at the warehouse, Joe is telling a dirty joke about a dumb Polack; all the others are present, including Mr Blue and Mr Brown. Joe turns his spiel around by telling 'em it's time to cut the jokes. As none of the six are personal friends, he imposes a rule that they are only to identify each other by their assigned colours. The Beard, 'Mr Pink', whines about his pseudonym until Joe makes it clear he has no choice.

Prior to the robbery, Freddy meets up with the black agent, who warns there will be no police presence unless the robbery gets out of hand. Freddy is edgy, complaining about the lack of protection. In a parallel scene, White talks him through the heist procedure, his part being to stand sentry over the doors.

Aftermath of robbery: repeat of screams heard post-credits. Brown is dying, with blood obscuring his vision. White opens up two .45s on a squad car, killing the cops inside. Freddy

Mr Pink (Steve Buscemi) at the armed robbery that goes disastrously wrong.

is dazed, White has to hustle him to move. White draws a pistol on a woman driver who panics and shoots a firearm from her glove compartment into Freddy's gut. Impulsively, Freddy blasts her through the head. White drags her from the car and carries the wounded Orange into the back. Freddy says the agonised words that open the movie, 'I can't believe she killed me.'

Warehouse: Eddie, White and Pink return, Eddie is shocked to find Vic dead. Orange groans out that he had to shoot him to save the mutilated cop, and Eddie, incensed, kills the patrolman instantly. Orange feeds him a line that Vic was planning them kill them all and make off with the haul; Eddie doesn't buy a word, saying Vic did four years when he could have bought himself out by naming his old man. As his temper boils over, Joe enters, accusing Orange of working with the LAPD. White, feeling responsible for the kid, insists it can't be so, and refuses to step out of the way for Joe to kill him. They go into a Western-style 'Mexican stand-off', where a slapstick exchange of bullets kills father and son and leaves White wounded. Pink crawls out of hiding and makes off with the cache of diamonds, followed by the wail of police sirens. The wounded White cradles the dying Orange's head in his lap, who confesses to being a cop. Defying police orders to drop his gun, White shoots Orange between the eyes, and is blown away in an offscreen fusillade of shots.

That the media was unprepared to be dazzled by such a modest little genre film, its standard plot submerged in layers of violent surprise and razor-sharp wise-ass dialogue (for credits see Appendix), is evident from the reaction that built up over the months after its premiere at the 1992 Cannes Film Festival. Tarantino had begun to refine the poetry of pulp cinema. 'If I hadn't made *Reservoir Dogs* and someone else had made it and I went and saw it, I'd think it was the best fuckin' movie of the year.'

The movie-maker's first time euphoria might have rung hollow, had it not been echoed by almost universal worldwide approval. One of the earliest *Dogs* reviews, by Leonard Klady in an April '92 issue of *Screen International*, stated, 'Only the film's graphic violence and language rein in a mainstream potential, suggesting strong specialised appeal of the order of David Lynch or Joel and Ethan Coen.' Perversely, while the movie's joyful aggression did prove a limiting factor back home, in the trigger-happy USA, the Brits took to it immediately. ('Should attract small but extremely devoted following eager to get in on the ground floor of the Next Big Thing,' said October's mini-review in the US *Premiere*, hitting it spot on as far as the mother country was concerned.)

Most significantly, *Dogs* never won a prize at that year's Sundance Festival, not because of its violent or profane content, but because the judges were so aware of insider reports that the movie was going to put its debutant director on the Hollywood 'A' list that they didn't believe he needed their help. Subsequent to the festival, distributors Miramax acquired the film, and it was on its way.

Within a few short months Tarantino leapfrogged the vast chasms that lay between the aspirations of a low-budget film director, acclaim as a cult movie auteur, and the status of an eminently quotable mass media entity, worthy of coverage in *Vanity Fair* and Andy Warhol's *Interview*. When the movie crossed the Atlantic in early '93, the fanfare that greeted its arrival was near deafening, sounded by the unlikeliest of trumpeters; even Julie Burchill – darling of London's ageing 'young fogey' set – could somehow declare *Dogs* to be 'the best film ever made', in contrast to her usual sideswipes against graphic murder scenes and 'boys' films'.

Clearly, both the movie and its fanboy director were cool; anyone who didn't testify to that end was in danger of missing the latest credibility boat.

Only the obscurity of the title prompted mild irritation. Some pundits decided it was a cryptogram to be deciphered, whereas the stark drama of the two mismatched words is an end in itself. Tarantino seemed to know the words 'reservoir' and 'dog' would symbiose into a stark image, far removed from mundane meaning – 'It's just a perfect title for those guys, they are Reservoir Dogs, whatever the hell that means.'

Whatever the phrase means, the characters – and the movie – got the thumbs-up from Connie, Tarantino's mother and most respected critic: 'They're just so male...'

The crooks

Mr White (Larry), played by Harvey Keitel. Larry is a rare item, a believable genre cliché. He's the thief with honour, the honest hold-up man who has principles and is gonna fuckin' stick to 'em. (A little street language serves to coarsen the old archetype.) Given credibility by Keitel's raw-edged performance, his paternal attitude toward youngblood Mr Orange (Tim Roth) is one of the pivotal devices of the movie. One short unfilmed section of Tarantino's original script (from which the movie was shot almost *verbatim*) suggests that Larry burst in and shot dead the undercover cop who infiltrated

Harvey Keitel as the principled Mr White.

his job before last. Orange's buddy could have become his nemesis in the click of a safety catch, but this doesn't happen till much too late (for Larry).

Feeling a sense of responsibility for the younger guy's agonising gut wound, Larry will neither run out on him, nor, when Joe Cabot fingers Orange as the 'rat in the house', dismiss his claim of comradeship. His sense of honour and duty towards his dying compadre is so great that it entails his own death. It seems a little above and beyond the call of duty – in fact, Larry's cradling of the dying Orange's head in his lap even seems more than a little faggy.

As Tarantino painstakingly sketches for us in the retrospectively unfolding plot, all these guys carry a lot of hard-earned history. Larry has done time, like most of them, so maybe he found himself looking at fresh-faced young cons with something more than a tough big-brother attitude. There again, if he dies purely and simply because he can't accept that he's wrong, he won't be the first; any pro criminal who walks around with a sense of self doubt would be too paralysed by inertia to act, or resist arrest. Larry may have found the anger and guns of the Cabot family easier to face than the recognition that he's been scammed, taken for a schmuck.

Keitel interprets the fatal buddy-buddy relationship between White and Orange in terms of 'mythological themes, universal themes of betrayal and redemption, and Mr White needed to be a hero to the younger man. And Mr Orange, who represents the law, has to seek redemption for carrying out what the law demands of him.'

Mr Orange (Freddy), played by British character actor Tim Roth. This youthful undercover cop is a swaggering cocksure runt, a believable two-dimensional character, and a great plot device. In character, Freddy fits the toothsome chirpiness of the little pothead hood like a glove, with not a shadow of law enforcement sticking to him. Playing inside a persona, conforming to or subverting expectation, is a major concern of Tarantino's. ('Let's get into character,' Jules, the assassin, says in the later *Pulp Fiction*.) As Freddy's superior, Holdaway, the black undercover, tells him, 'An undercover cop has got to be Marlon Brando.' It calls to mind the ear-biting undercover cop, Mick Belker, and the cast of misfits he effortlessly impersonated, in *Hill Street Blues*. It also stresses that the persona is everything; that as a hood, Freddy/Orange can really be said to exist within the story, whereas as a cop he's the invisible man. Only when he pumps lead into Mr Blonde does the hand of the law assert itself through him, and even then, it's only possible while the others are out of the room and his mask has slipped. It's a tribute to Roth, performing with a creditably nasal accent, that we see recognition of his own culpability build up in his face. Larry's massacre of the squad car cops leaves him stunned, resigned to his own impotence; moments later, the killing of the innocent woman driver, as an instinctive response to his own wounding, means that he's just as guilty as any of them.

By the time of the last-minute revelation of his identity to Larry, he has much to confess. 'I swear on my mother's eternal soul, that's what happened,' he squealed when trying to explain the killing of Blonde. From that point the movie is almost in a hysteria-pitch parallel to Scorsese's – cop or not, the boy's sin demands redemption or retribution, but there's no priest to confess to, only Larry. He might have died easy with the knowledge that he only did bad on behalf of the good guys. But, in his hood persona, Larry was his friend, and all it adds up to is another betrayal.

Mr Blonde ('Toothpick Vic' Vega to his friends), played by Michael Madsen. An imposingly physical but initially subdued presence, and a professional of an entirely different temperament. He is implicitly trusted by the father-and-son business of Joe and Eddie Cabot, for whom he served four years without turning state's evidence to get himself off. The first impression made by Mr Blonde, in the pre-credits coffee house scene, is that he's a big mother who looks like he can handle himself; the second is that he's a gentleman, relatively speaking, among a pretty mean and foul-mouthed bunch. He takes the conventional line on Madonna's song, 'Like a Virgin', a real bone of contention to the garrulous Mr Brown (Tarantino himself), who insists the girl's singing about an insatiable girl who meets a stud hung like the late porn star Big John Holmes, and 'she's feeling something she ain't felt since forever – pain'. Vic Vega, the old romantic, can't believe it's about anything other than a vulnerable girl who meets a sensitive guy and experiences love for the first time. Similarly, he takes big issue with Mr Pink in the cafe when he argues they shouldn't tip the waitress, asking indignantly, 'Do you know what these ladies make?' Vic's a real stand-up guy – until the (unseen) robbery, when much of the chaos that occurs is down to him losing his cool and blasting off at the wholesaler's clerks for daring to sound the alarm. Holed up in the warehouse, White and Pink curse him for turning the job into a bulletfest, bemoaning his gratuitous murder of a young black woman. ('I don't even know what gratuitous means,' he jokes to his terrorised cop victim.)

Larry is wound up to breaking point by Vic's attitude, but there's a sense that, despite all the screamed threats, he's unnerved by a guy who can act so insanely and remain so calm. As Tarantino says, 'Some switch got flipped in prison,' and none of his 'co-workers' can anticipate the extremity of his behaviour. By the time of the film's most infamous scene, the torture of patrolman Marvin Nash, Vic/Blonde has become one of the most stylish, memorable and scarily convincing screen villains ever.

Mr Pink, played by Steve Buscemi. A wired, goatee-bearded true survivor, Pink is always an audience's most despised character – for not seeming as tough as the others, for being edgy to the point of irritability, for slithering away with the loot, for being on the lower end of the famous stand-off with Mr White, or for simply refusing to tip the waitress.

His creator has a lot more sympathy for him. Pink is placed as a kind of manic Jiminy Cricket on the shoulders of the other characters, reminding them of how much shit they're in and how they ought to take evasive action. He's the first to insist a snitch led to the cops being in position to gun down Messrs Brown and Blue; he tells White the job's too fucked-up to stick to existing plans, that they ought to quit the warehouse and split the takings; his attitude to Orange may be heartless, as the promise of a crooked surgeon to take the slug from the kid's gut is White's only tie to the rendezvous area, but, in terms of survival instinct, he's 100 percent right. He also screams at White for being dumb enough to reveal his true identity to Orange – like Tarantino says, 'Everything he says is right, he just doesn't have the courage of his own convictions.'

Tarantino also uses the character to air some of his own grievances about life on the bottom rung. Pink's firm conviction that compulsory tipping is one of society's

Mr Blonde (Michael Madsen) watches the argument between Mr White and Mr Pink.

cheaper con tricks may seem like the petty whining of a tightwad, but, to anyone who's spent any time on Shit Street, it's a recognisable, if mean-spirited sentiment: 'That was my credo for years,' says Tarantino. 'Because when I was making minimum wage, no-one was tipping me. I didn't have a job that society deemed tip-worthy.'

Later, while going into paranoid overdrive (this guy is nervous – he drinks six cups of coffee for breakfast), Pink draws a parallel between the unease he felt about the heist, and scoring dope: 'Every time I ever got burned buying weed, I always knew the guy wasn't right... But I wanted to believe him. If he's not lyin' to me, and it really is Thai stick, then whoa baby. But it's never Thai stick.' Like half of his generation, marijuana competes with alcohol for Tarantino's recreational drug of choice. But when you're a nobody among nobodies, as Tarantino once was, 'it's never Thai stick' is a pretty sharp analogy for the way life always is.

It's no surprise to hear that Tarantino originally intended to play Pink, his alter ego, himself. Another nearly-ran was Dennis Hopper, who was bowled over by the script when Keitel showed it to him, but was already committed to another film.

When last glimpsed, Pink is scurrying away with a briefcase full of diamonds while all about him lie dead and dying, calling to mind the grizzled old boy played by Walter Huston in *The Treasure of the Sierra Madre*, who also had the self-preservation instincts of a reservoir rat. When asked whether he felt his character escaped destruction by staying aloof from the other men, Steve Buscemi said: 'I don't think he is a loner... He was told not to get to know these other guys, and he takes his job very seriously... He is the most professional and that's why he is a survivor.'

Nice Guy Eddie, played by Chris Penn. Chunky, solid underworld sonny boy. Dependable, if you're working in the same arena as him, dedicated to his friends and his 'Daddy'. Quick to anger, violent, even murderous, but the Nice Guy tag is not meant to be ironic, all things being relative: his nickname is a tribute to his more sociable qualities. A secondary but fairly authentic character.

Joe Cabot, played by Lawrence Tierney. Eddie's father, a likeable old hoodlum, old-fashioned, reciprocating loyalty where it's shown (to psychotic Vic Vega). Also belligerent, bloated, bigoted, and merciless when crossed, just like his job description says he ought to be.

Mr Blue, played by Eddie Bunker, a genuine former real-life hood of the old school. Not given much more to do than look menacing, and add a little comedy by coming on as the world's oldest, craggiest Madonna expert in the pre-credits sequence. There's still more cross-pollination between Tarantino and Bunker than meets the eye (see page 40).

Mr Brown, played by Tarantino. The smartass who thinks Madonna's as big a slut as she puts out to be. Brown exists to articulate the dirty-minded theory on 'Like a

Virgin' that has stuck in everyone's memory, to allow his creator a small part in his own movie, and to die violently.

Tarantino has expressed his desire to create a personal universe of archetypal characters. One of his methods is to have certain figures cross-referenced from one film to another. In *Dogs*, Marsellus – an underworld figure known to Joe Cabot – is mentioned as being away on a long stretch; in *Pulp Fiction*, Marsellus Wallace is a central character. Mr Blonde's real name, as revealed in the flashback when he's fresh out of prison and comes to meet Joe, is Vic Vega; in *Pulp Fiction*,

Lawrence Tierney

the junkie hitman played by John Travolta is named Vincent Vega, in a part originally offered to Michael Madsen.

Using characters as signposts across his personal universe is a device the new-crowned King of Pulp copped from J. D. Salinger, author of *The Catcher in the Rye* and a literary favourite of Tarantino's. Salinger's knack of making well-crafted dialogue sound conversational, almost throwaway, is a strong influence on his fan.

So why did *Reservoir Dogs* occasion all the positive hysteria?

In the film Tarantino didn't just play with the crime movie genre; he defined it as a set of predicaments, a trap, locking a handful of sharply defined characters into that trap and letting them fight it out to the death.

He credits his 'forced perspectives' with keeping the audience engaged in the action, having ensured both the narrative and the camera take an 'odd point of view': 'When the movie's getting ready to take a left turn, the audience starts leaning to the left; when it's getting ready to make a right turn, the audience moves to the right; when it's supposed to suck 'em in, they move up close... you just know what's gonna happen. You don't know you know, but you know.

'Admittedly there's a lot of fun in playing against that, fucking up the breadcrumb trail that we don't even know we're following, using an audience's own subconscious preconceptions against them so they actually have a viewing experience, they're actually involved in the movie.' Cameras pan, perspectives shift – what's out of view is just as important as what's in shot. Reality is a subjective, ever-changing chimera.

'In the first section, up until Mr Orange shoots Mr Blonde, the characters have far more information about what's going on than you have – and they have conflicting information. Then the Mr Orange sequence happens and that's a great leveller. You start getting caught up with exactly what's going on, and in the third part, when you go back into the warehouse for the climax you are totally ahead of everybody – you know far more than any one of the characters. You know more than Keitel, Buscemi and Penn, because you know that Mr Orange is a cop and you know more than Mr Orange does because he's got his own little ruse he's gonna say but you know Mr Blonde's lineage, you know he went to jail for four years for Chris Penn's father, you know what Chris Penn knows. And when Mr White is pointing the gun at Joe and saying, "You're wrong about this man," you know he's right.'

The development of Freddy's cover story moves from the awkward coaching by Holdaway (the black LAPD detective) to word-perfect rehearsal in front of the mirror, and finally to detail-perfect improvisation with Joe Cabot & Co. The way he talks himself into his 'cops in the commode' story, positioned as the narrator, gives a personalised slant on the lies inherent in the film's narrative. Lies, in this instance, are just another take on reality, and are as good as any other character's truth. Tarantino has acknowledged the influence of Akira Kurosawa's *Rashomon* which tells the same story from four very different standpoints.

Holdaway's advice to Freddy, about making the story his own and knowing every dirty inch of the crapper where it takes place, could possibly have come from the back of Tarantino's subconscious mind, where he's stored every hardboiled crime genre convention and scenario, making ready to bring a set of pulp fiction archetypes into the real world he inhabits.

While *Dogs* was wringing praise out of even the most jaded, some audience members picked up on the idea that it was a movie with its basis in experience of 'living the life'. Real fun for real hoodlums – so it seemed to them. The facts of the matter are trickier, and it's a tribute to Tarantino's sleight of hand. He's very aware of playing a game that offsets brute realism against cinematic stylisation – 'I get a kick out of doing that. There's realism and there's movie-movie-ness,' – though he's loathe to deny the presence of a more visceral kind of truth.

Dogs' language follows the blueprint made by Brian DePalma's 1983 remake of *Scarface*, starring Al Pacino as the modern Al Capone, a Cuban coke dealer who gets scolded by his squeeze, Michelle Pfeiffer, for saying 'fuck' every other word. Scarface remains the model for the modern American gangster film – frenetic, foul-mouthed, violent almost to the point of absurdity. Its director, Brian De Palma, is a Tarantino hero.

Obscenity has a potency of its own, but it's not the be-all and end-all. Tarantino knows conversational rhythm carries its own credibility. Nice Guy Eddie tells his warehouse dogs to stop beating up Patrolman Nash, saying, 'You beat on this prick enough, he'll tell ya he started the Chicago fire. That don't necessarily make it so.' 'What you gotta do is break that son-of-a-bitch in two,' says Larry, advising of the way to treat the diamond wholesale managers. 'If you wanna know something and he won't tell you, cut off one of his fingers... Then you tell 'im his thumb's next. After that he'll tell ya if he wears ladies' underwear.'

Both statements are born of black expediency, both carry a grim profundity, and –

most of all – have a rhythm harking back to the darkest of the post-war dimestore pulp crime writers.

Stacey Sher, President of Jersey Films, Danny De Vito's production company which took on *Pulp Fiction*, tells the following story: 'Quentin told me... about when he was little, and he'd be playing with his GI Joes, making up things, and saying all these outrageous things, and his mom would say, "Quentin, don't use that kind of language!", and he would say, "It's not me, Mom, it's the characters. It's the guys, that's what they'd say."'

When profanity and the rhythm of pulp are married to attitude, it's a powerful mixture. 'Fuckin' jungle bunny goes out there, slits some old woman's throat for 25 cents. Fuckin' nigger gets Doris Day as a parole officer,' opines Joe Cabot, in the authoritative voice of the old school American 'made man'. It's a great line – bigoted, banal, rhythmic, funny. Anyone who thinks Tarantino's thrown it in to freak out the politically correct is missing the point – this is how a guy like Joe thinks, and his scriptwriter had better find an amusing way of expressing it. Later in the same scene, when Nice Guy Eddie and Toothpick Vic are goading each other like the reunited best friends they are, Vic jokes that Eddie would have been made into a sore-assed whore if he'd done time in the same place: 'I'd be makin' you my dog's bitch – you'd be suckin' the dick and goin' down on a mangy T-bone hound.' The sheer poetry offends Eddie, though he has to respond just as jokily, with a jibe about Vic 'talkin' like a nigger', with his brain contaminated by the black man's semen he's taken up his ass.

We're feasting on two aspects of prison paranoia here – the 'jocker and punk' syndrome, where homosexual rape is used not only as an outlet for sexual frustration, but as a means of establishing a hierarchy; where the power is wielded by the 'pitcher' who 'rips off the punk's ass', who is not considered a 'faggot', while the 'catcher', who takes it, willing or not, certainly is.

The other major fear is racial; if a young white male heterosexual worries about being subjugated as a punk/bitch, there's an extra element of fear involved in being physically invaded by someone who wants to dominate your ass, your soul and your race. Eddie and Vic make a joke of it; but they know what it is to do time; and, like their creator, Tarantino, they're jokily articulating the kind of fear realistically expressed in Eddie Bunker's *The Animal Factory*.

Reservoir Dogs chimes bells of authenticity with many viewers, but its realism is based on a pop-culture sensibility. We recognise these doomed hoods as stepping out of the collective consciousness formed by the movies and TV shows we've watched over the years; by the paperbacks and comic books we've read; even by the records and radio shows we've heard. Their behaviour is that of fictional archetypes exiled into the real world, forced to abide by some of its rules.

One of the most potent devices for audience identification is the radio show that permeates much of the movie, *K-Billy's Sounds of the 70s*, first introduced in the pre-credits sequence by Nice Guy Eddie, when he waxes nostalgic over the murder ballad 'The Night the Lights Went Out in Georgia'. K-Billy himself, personified by the largactyl tones of comedian Steven Wright, is a real junk culture arbiter. (Giveaway prizes on the

Eddie Bunker

Born in Hollywood, 1938, to stagehand father and chorus girl mother. Made a ward of the state after his parents' divorce when he was four. After stints in reform school and youth prison, befriended Louise Fazenda Wallis, wife of Hal Wallis (producer of *Casablanca*), who tried to steer him straight. But sentenced to year in county jail, aged 16, when caught with marijuana after LA car chase ending in multi-car pile-up; at 17, sentenced for violation of parole terms. Served four and a half years, during which time he read voraciously, and wrote on a typewriter provided by Louise Wallis.

Eddie Bunker

Organised armed robberies and ran a protection racket, then served seven years for passing forged cheque. During this period, wrote four novels and many short stories, often selling blood to pay for postage; on release, arrested for robbing floor safe in a bar; feigning schizophrenia, sent to Vacaville Prison for the Criminally Insane; eventually standing trial, he made bail, using freedom to build up 'a little drug empire'; caught robbing a bank by narcotics agents who bugged his car; sentenced to concurrent five/six-year sentences. While awaiting trial, his first novel, *No Beast So Fierce*, was accepted for publication – the story of a long-term prisoner trying to integrate into society, who finds he can't live as the repentant unemployed ex-con he's expected to be, and erupts into a raging one-man crime wave. Wrote second novel, *The Animal Factory*, in Marion Prison, Illinois, telling of a young drug dealer who kills to save his ass from rape in San Quentin. In 1977 he met Dustin Hoffman, who had read his first novel and hoped to make it into a film; it became *Straight Time*, a worthy adaptation starring Hoffman as Bunker's anti-hero, Max Dembo.

Eddie Bunker was released from prison in 1975, and has remained a free man ever since. In 1985 he co-wrote the screenplay for Konchalovsky's thriller, *Runaway Train*, a critical and commercial hit which earned an Oscar nomination for its star, Jon Voight, playing an escaped prisoner.

Whatever the reason for his casting, Eddie Bunker makes an indelible visual impression, with his hawk eyes, liver spots and sceptical expression. It may well be that Tarantino borrowed more from his writing than is acknowledged, though there's no doubt he reciprocated in kind. In 1993, the year of *Reservoir Dogs*' UK release, the crime publishers, No Exit Press, launched a series of Bunker reprints on the back of a plug by Tarantino for *No Beast So Fierce*. As Bunker asserts, Tarantino studied *Straight Time* while shooting the preparatory rushes of his debut at the Sundance Institute. It seems to have part-inspired the stitching of faultless lowlife dialogue into an otherwise highly stylised movie.

show include tickets to a 'Monster Truck Extravaganza', a kind of automotive alternative to all-in wrestling or *Gladiators*.)

'I love the use of music in movies,' says Tarantino. '*Ride of the Valkyries* has been around for a hundred years, but I defy anyone not to think of *Apocalypse Now* when they hear that piece of music. And when I hear the opening strands of the Ronettes' 'Be My Baby', I see Harvey Keitel's head hit the pillow in *Mean Streets*. In LA you have a lot of oldie stations and they have special weekends – a Motown weekend, a Beatles weekend – so I came up with the idea of a Super 70s weekend. I didn't want to go for the serious stuff – Led Zeppelin or Marvin Gaye – I wanted to go for the super sugary 70s bubblegum sound. One, because some people are annoyed by it and, two, because I grew up with it. The sugariness of it, the catchiness of it, really lightens up a rude, rough movie.'

Some of the immediately recognisable songs are used sardonically – Harry Nilsson's 'Coconut' ends the movie, a mock-calypso with the refrain: 'Doctor! / Is there nothing I can take? / I say DOCTOR! / To relieve this bellyache?'; the most celebrated number, Stealer's Wheel's 'Stuck in the Middle with You' is, as K-Billy says, 'Dylanesque bubblegum', a 1974 flare-flapper from the folk rock outfit featuring Gerry Rafferty, formerly half of folk duo The Humblebums (with Billy Connolly), and composer of the late 70s hit with the asthmatic sax motif, 'Baker Street'. The featured song is a less

Mr Brown (Quentin Tarantino), Mr Blonde (Michael Madsen) and Mr Blue (Eddie Bunker) discussing Madonna's ethics.

wordy take on Bob Dylan's more light-hearted surreal numbers, like 'Stuck Inside of Mobile with the Memphis Blues Again', though the lyrics bear a passing resemblance to Randy Newman's 'Mama Told Me Not to Come' (a big 1970 hit for Three Dog Night, *Sounds of the 70s* fans). Mr Blonde makes a macabre play on the lead-in lines, 'Clowns to the left of me / Jokers to the right / Here I am...' By the time he returns to the warehouse with a can of gasoline, Gerry Rafferty is reaching the middle section of the song, where he sings, 'Ple-ee-ee-ee-ee-ease!' in a falsetto, stressing Patrolman Nash's predicament almost unbearably.

Mr Brown's blaspheming against the secular Madonna, in the pre-credits coffee house sequence, has become near-legendary, confirming Tarantino has more to say about pop culture than about bullet wounds. Ms Ciccone was tolerance itself, considering the script referred to the girl singing the song as a regular 'fuck machine', shrugging it off when every face at the screening she attended turned to her for a reaction. After all, this was a movie that treated her nouveau Marilyn/sex-bitch career with respect, with six armed men arguing over the highlights of her repertoire before setting out on a robbery.

'You know, Madonna liked the movie a lot and wanted to meet me,' says Tarantino. 'So I asked her, "Am I right about the song?" because I really believed that was the subtext. She said, "No, it's about love, it's about a girl who's been messed over and finally meets this one man who loves her." She signed my *Erotica* album, "To Quentin. It's not about dick, it's about love. Madonna."'

Dogs is signposted with a few pop culture references that mean more to Tarantino than to the characters voicing them. When Freddy/Orange is psyching himself up in the mirror, he tells himself he's the TV detective Baretta. On the wall of his apartment is a poster for *The Silver Surfer*, one of Tarantino's favourite comic books. Describing Joe Cabot, he compares him to the comic book character The Thing – formerly Ben Grimm, a cosmically mutated fighter pilot who resembled a mobile gravel pit and formed part of *The Fantastic Four*, his stock periodically boosted by battles with his more popular counterpart, *The Incredible Hulk*; likely or not, Officer Holdaway gets it straight away. Spinning the yarn about how he became the local weed man on his manor, Freddy complains that he couldn't even rent a tape without getting bugged by phone calls – 'Motherfucker, I'm tryin' to watch *Lost Boys*.' Now, while slobbing out with video cassettes is almost a universal vice, even with hoods (or cops pretending to be hoods), what's of little importance to these guys is remembering what movies they've seen, leave alone specific titles. In these instances, Orange is not just a plot device or a harbinger of doom, he's a cultural spokesman for Tarantino, just as Pink is his social mouthpiece.

'The movie doesn't stop for the references to be flagged,' claims Tarantino, 'so if you're just a regular viewer, you're just following the movie and you're emotionally involved in it. If you're a film geek who does get it, that's fine, that's cool; but the movie doesn't stop for you to get it... I don't do in-jokes... You know, you're watching a horror movie: "Hey Detective Romero, meet Commissioner Argento." That gives me a headache.'

Assault on Precinct 13 *(1976), John Carpenter's tense action movie, observes the attack by a mixed-race urban guerilla group on an undermanned police station. Tarantino has cited the movie as an influence on the making of* Reservoir Dogs, *which is at least a tone or two darker. While both* Precinct 31 *and* Rio Bravo *have their protagonists facing up to an overwhelming state of siege from 'out there', Tarantino's bickering anti-heroes are under attack from within. By the time the cops actually converge on the warehouse, everyone has been destroyed by betrayal, suspicion and misjudgment.*

The Thing *(1982), like* Precinct 13, *marks John Carpenter as a Howard Hawks for more uncertain times. Unlike its prototype –* The Thing *(1951), directed by Christian Nyby under a firm guiding hand from producer Hawks – Carpenter's version has an alien monster attacking a polar ice station's occupants from within. Tarantino has said he wanted to translate the paranoia of* The Thing's *characters, all fighting the enemy within, into a more realistic milieu for* Reservoir Dogs.

Tarantino also has no time for homages. 'I steal from everything. Great artists steal, they don't do homages.' He said this in answer to the accusation that the plot of *Reservoir Dogs* bears an uncanny resemblance to the last 20 minutes of Hong Kong heist movie *City on Fire* (1989). 'It's a great movie. I steal from every single movie ever made.'

Reservoir Dogs may not call a halt to pay lip service to its closest ancestors such as *The Taking of Pelham 1-2-3*, *The Asphalt Jungle* or *City on Fire*, but Tarantino never passes up any small opportunity to shout out his love of the reel thing. For example, the climactic Mexican stand-off – where the doomed faces of the three hoods burn with operatic rage – recalls (along with the more recent *City on Fire*) the spaghetti westerns of Sergio Leone. The unblinking exchange of bullets, where Larry, Joe and Eddie all manage to shoot each other simultaneously, pays tribute to the mute arias of staring, sweat and silence that form the gun duel scenes of *The Good, The Bad and The Ugly*, and *Once Upon a Time in the West*.

The shoot-out's comic outcome also presents an unanswered puzzle: Who shot Nice Guy Eddie? 'It's in the shot,' answers Tarantino unhelpfully, knowing that an apparently in-built continuity fault gives the fans something else to get obsessive about. Let's work it out by logical process of elimination: Mr White shoots face-on at Joe, not his son, and is only seen to fire one of his two barettas. Mr Orange has emptied all his bullets on Mr Blonde, and is not seen to reload, or to be holding a handgun after the shootings. This leaves us with – Mr Pink. Pink is kept out of frame for a long time, up to and beyond the Mexican stand-off; after the three-way shooting has ended, and all have hit the deck (Eddie falling forward, as if hit from behind), Pink crawls out from under a ramp

Mr Orange lets rip into 'Toothpick Vic' Vega after he has cut off the cop's ear.

holding his gun, which he stashes away while making off with the diamonds – the ultimate reservoir rat survivor.

A final reference is a borrowing from Tarantino's favourite war movie, Brian de Palma's 1989 Vietnam crime-and-punishment melodrama, *Casualties of War*. The style, tone and substance of Mr White's attempt to reassure the dying Mr Orange derive from the way one of *Casualties'* characters (Sergeant Meserve) consoles a mortally wounded colleague, refusing to accept his claim that he's dying: 'Look in my eyes. You are not fuckin' dyin'.'

The setpiece that springs to the mind of the casual viewer, whenever the title *Reservoir Dogs* comes up, is the musically accompanied torture of Patrolman Nash by Mr Blonde. '*Reservoir Dogs* turned up in the catalogue of the Sundance Film Festival, and I was there for the first screening of it,' recalls Todd McCarthy, chief film critic for *Variety*, 'and it was a stunning experience, because most the guys in the audience were absolutely riveted by the film, and there were quite a few walk-outs at the predictable ear scene, and all of the walk-outs were women. So it was obvious this was a film that would have its die-hard adherents, as well as people who just couldn't take it.' Incongrously, one of those who walked out during this scene was Wes Craven, writer/director of classic splatter movie *The Hills Have Eyes*, and creator of the cuddliest deformed paedophile ghoul in town, Freddie Krueger. Craven's first feature, *The Last House on the Left*, had them rushing for the exit.

Tarantino wasn't slow to present his side of the case (though he's since said he never wants to talk about the violence in *Dogs* again): 'To say that I get a big kick out of violence in movies and can enjoy violence in movies but find it totally abhorrent in real life – I can feel totally justified and totally comfortable with that statement. I do not think that one is a contradiction of the other... I love that scene. I love what it does cinematically, emotionally, performance-wise. To me it's the most cinematic scene in the whole movie.'

The complaint against it seems due to its effectiveness – the boy is making us hurt all over again. That the average TNT-powered action picture has a far higher body count needs no arguing, but Tarantino's gore is personal: small-scale, intimate, claustrophobic.

In reality the violence of *Reservoir Dogs* is a lot less graphic than it feels. The torture scene takes its cue from *The Texas Chainsaw Massacre*, the least bloody of splatter masterpieces. By the time Mr Blonde is bumping and grinding through 'Stuck in the Middle with You', razor in hand, we can believe we'll see just about anything. As the screaming cop's ear is cut off, the squeamish avert their eyes, but by then the camera has already diverted its own gaze, giving a face-on view of the warehouse wall. By the time those sensitive souls are looking back at the screen, they're faced by Blonde whispering, 'Was that as good for you as it was for me?' into the severed organ. What's seen is a pulse quickener, but it's what's implied that is more than some people can bear.

While driving around San Fernando Valley in the Geo he bought with his *True Romance* money, Tarantino caught a radio news report quoting LA's Catholic Archbishop condemning the current wave of violence in movies. Said the announcer, 'While the controversy continues to boil, along comes a film that exceeds all previous

Mr White and Mr Pink square up for another confrontation in the warehouse, in front of the trussed-up Patrolman Nash (Kirk Baltz).

films when it comes to violence. It's so graphic that dozens of repulsed viewers fled from early screenings...'

With a dawning sense of realisation, Tarantino recognised that was his baby they were talking about. '*Reservoir Dogs* is a total talkfest,' he protested at the time, 'a bunch of guys yakking at one another. And then once in a while there's a little bit of violence.'

When filmed talking with Brian De Palma, for the BBC's *Hollywood's Boy Wonder* documentary, he reflected on the furore: 'One of the things you've said, that I've used in different interviews, 'cos it was so right on the money, is that as a filmmaker, when you deal in violence you're penalised for doing a good job. I know people who could have seen *Reservoir Dogs* and been absolutely fine with it, but when they hear "VIOLENCE! VIOLENCE! VIOLENCE!"... They talked about *Reservoir Dogs* as if it was one of the most violent... the most violent movie ever made. Now some day, I may make the most violent movie ever made and I won't mind people saying it – but I didn't. I'm imagining I'm the husband of some young couple, and we're just sitting there, and the thing is: "What do you want to see tonight, honey? Do you want to see *Forrest Gump*?" "Well, what's that?" "That's the movie with Tom Hanks playing the retarded guy who meets John F. Kennedy." "Oh, okay. What else?" "Or *Clear and Present Danger*." "What's that?" "That's the new Harrison Ford movie. Or do you want to see *Reservoir Dogs*?"

"What's that?" "Well that's the movie where the guy gets his ear cut off."' (De Palma cracked up with laughter at this point.)

One more movie down the line, the *Dogs* director had the offending scene placed neatly in context, as an intense piece of dramatic ritual: 'The thing that I am really proud of in the torture scene in *Dogs*... is the fact that it's truly funny up until the point that he cuts the cop's ear off. While he's up there doing that little dance to 'Stuck in the Middle with You', I pretty much defy anybody to watch and not enjoy it... And then when he starts cutting the ear off, that's not played for laughs. The cop's pain is not played like one big joke, it's played for real. And then after that when he makes a joke, when he starts talking into the ear, that gets you laughing again. So now you've got his coolness and his dance, the joke of talking into the ear and the cop's pain, they're all tied up together. And that's why I think that scene caused such a sensation, because you don't know how you're supposed to feel when you see it.'

In the UK, the politically empowered British Board of Film Classification refused to grant *Reservoir Dogs* a certificate for video release. With the nation still reeling at the time of its theatrical release from the murder of a two-year-old child by two disturbed young schoolboys, society's kneejerk elements screamed for simple solutions, particularly the banning of violent video films.

Where exactly *Dogs* fits into the backlash is almost a mystery, with no suggestion that either of the murderous children saw (impossible at the time) or was affected by its content. BBFC boss James Ferman made a political compromise, claiming a certificate

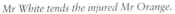

Mr White tends the injured Mr Orange.

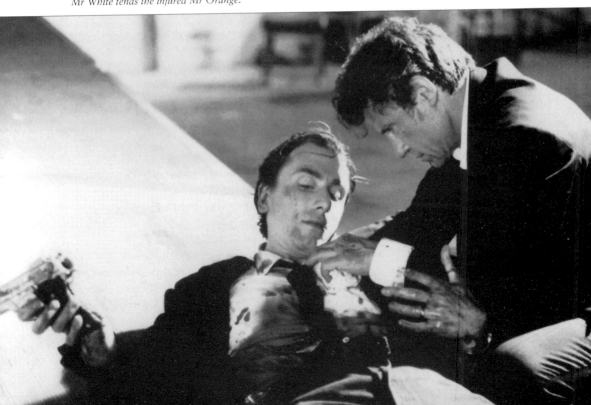

had been 'delayed', rather than denied, until a more appropriate time for release. (The film's video release took place in June 1995, delayed from the scheduled July 1993.)

The tabloid press tried to keep the controversy going on the week of the movie's British video release: 'Reservoir Dog boy aged 14 led copycat gun rampage,' ran a headline. The papers quoted the prosecution as stating that a South London juvenile and his older accomplice had watched *Dogs* and snorted poppers before robbing two newsagents with an imitation pistol, almost offering them a plea of mitigating circumstances.

Tarantino is unmoved by any accusation of his debut feature being a corrupting influence: 'You could even make the case that *Dogs* ultimately ended up being very moralistic. I never intended it to be this way, but in some ways my films go by the old Hays Code. You can do anything you want in the first 88 minutes as long as in the last two minutes there's some retribution for what the characters have done. I never set out to do that. I always thought if I wrote a heist film, I'd do one where they all got away. But it didn't quite work out that way.'

It's often claimed that the movie's characters inhabit an amoral universe, but as their creator says, the movie's pay-off puts the lie to that. Morality is imposed by the situation itself; distrust and confusion breed the only conceivable end. These guys all live within an amoral subculture, but they're stuck in a universe that imposes mortality – crushes the innocent, kills innocent bystanders, but saves the most poetic fates for the wiseacres who think they can beat the world at its own vicious game. Justice comes from elsewhere, in the manner that pulps and 'B' movies imposed order on violence for many years, or the way in which 1950s horror comics ensured every wrongdoer came to an ironically gory end.

Tarantino has refused to embroil himself in the censorship argument – he praises his 'fantastic dealings' with the MPAA, the USA's ratings board – even in the country (the UK) where his movie was most popular, and where, for two-and-a-half years, it could not be released on video.

Dogs' cult status in Europe served to pull in more bucks than its 'ultraviolent' reputation in the USA. 'The movie grossed three million in the US,' says Lawrence Bender, 'and we've figured the movie only cost a million-and-a-half bucks. To me that's successful.' '*Reservoir Dogs* wasn't that well received in the States, it certainly did much better here,' contradicts early Tarantino supporter and confirmed friend Terry Gilliam. (Overall, the movie has taken about 20 million in sterling, much of it in Europe, of which about six million is in Britain.) 'I thought Quentin's great success was that he then went to Cannes, then he went for a year on the film festival circuit, garnering more publicity than anyone I've seen in the last several years.'

Beginning with *Dogs*' Euro-debut at Cannes, its creator hit the festival circuit, leaving California for the first time in years, and the USA for the first time in his life. Hyped on adrenalin, and with first impressions of foreign cities seen through pop-culture eyes, these new stimuli began to spark off the fanboy archive of movie imagery in his head.

CHAPTER 3

True romance – 'I wanted to be that hillbilly'

There was one other pitstop on the way to creating an undisputed classic. An enjoyable detour, due to belated production of the first script ever written by the new-crowned king geek.

'I wrote it to be this big, flashy, show-offy first film,' recalls Tarantino of the *True Romance* screenplay, now firmly in the habit of attributing writer's credit entirely to himself, forgetting Roger Avary's contribution. 'I was going to direct it and Roger [Avary] was going to produce it. We were going to try to be the Coen brothers, with him in Ethan's job and me in Joel's job. We were going to try to raise, like, $1.2 million. We never even considered taking it to a studio. They wouldn't like it and they wouldn't let me direct it.'

As already stated (see chapter 1), the script found its way to Hollywood businessman Stanley Margolis, via agent Cathryn James.

'This guy is, like, "It's great. It's wonderful. In maybe three months we can get the money for this, and then in six months we can be in pre-production on it and stuff. Quentin, you'll direct, no problem." Me and Roger left the building and just proceeded to have an orgasm. We walked to our car and we're just hugging each other and just, like, over the moon. "We're gonna do it! This was so easy! This is going to be so great!" It was one of the most euphoric moments of my life.'

When first expressing faith in Tarantino and Avary's script, Margolis told them it was too good to try to film 'guerilla-style' in 16mm on a budget of $60,000, as was their original intent. Eventually, he'd take the bold step of mortgaging his house to try to raise a $2.7 million budget, after seemingly every production company in the business had turned it down on the basis of the insistence that Tarantino – still then unknown – be the director.

'It just proceeded to completely stall for three years,' Tarantino says, recalling how he came back to earth with a bump. 'It was like this whole thing where, "Oh, in two weeks we'll know for sure." Two weeks, two weeks, two weeks, two weeks, forever. A year and a half of two weeks. Finally, about midway through, they said, "Quentin, if you step down we could get it going really quick. You're the problem." By this point, I didn't care about it any more. I just wanted the money, because I was flat-busted broke. So I stepped down.'

Stanley Margolis initially put forward exploitation movie director William Lustig to helm the project, with Tarantino's full agreement. Lustig had late-80s success with the horror movie *Maniac Cop*, and was infamous for his similarly titled but much grimmer 1980 debut, *Maniac*, a nihilistic killer's-eye-view slasher movie, with gruesome effects by Tom Savini and a clammy title performance by screenwriter Joe Spinnell. The initial enthusiasm was to die, however, when it became clear Lustig was fascinated but bemused by Tarantino's manic, talky script, and the movie geek himself refused to give way to suggestions for making *True Romance* into standard exploitation fare. Strangely, for the man who directed *Maniac* – which made Craven's *Last House on the Left* look like *ET*, in terms of critical and audience response – Lustig decided such an eccentrically cultish little script couldn't live without a happy ending. Clearly, he'd adjusted to the realpolitik of the movie industry over the previous decade.

Tarantino was unhappy, as his original ending had the main female character, Alabama Whitman, mourning her husband Clarence, shot dead in the movie's climactic gunplay. Somehow, the trajectory of the two desperate lovers seemed to demand it, much as the doomed-lovers-on-the-road movies that served as his inspiration ended with the downfall of their central characters. Despite his penchant for plundering genres while discarding the corresponding clichés, the projects remaining in Tarantino's own hands retained an ironically moral flavour – something the director of *True Romance* would jettison, thereby cuing knee-jerk outrage from the moral minority.

'At the stage where we finally did the deal,' remembers Stanley Margolis, 'the foreign distributors wanted the ending rewritten to make it more upbeat. Quentin refused, but Roger rewrote it for them. It was perfect because he had collaborated with Quentin all the way through.'

Avary added a narrative voice-over by Alabama, describing how she rescued Clarence, who she'd believed dead, and how he recovered and ran away with her to a fairy tale island, where they lived happily ever after and fathered a son named after Clarence's (and Tarantino's) hero, Elvis. (When the script was finally filmed, baby Elvis was played by the three-year-old son of Patricia Arquette, the actress who played Alabama.)

Reassured by the audience-friendly amoral ending – most young moviegoers would sympathise with two likeable kids who hit the jackpot with a single big cocaine deal, whatever the moral implications – and set to tamper with the order of the non-chronological narrative, Lustig bought the script from Tarantino for $30,000. (By now, despite the still-active involvement of the mildly compliant Avary, *True Romance* was being hawked as 'written by Quentin Tarantino'.) The Writers' Guild minimum payment would act as seed money for *Reservoir Dogs* (until Harvey Keitel came to the rescue – see chapter 2), and Lustig could do whatever he liked with the script. However, there was no final 'done deal', and negotiations were not over; despite messy litigation, Bill Lustig would never bring his planned version of *True Romance* to the screen.

Margolis next struck a deal with Samuel Hadida, a Paris-based producer. Hadida took the script to August Entertainment in 1991, months prior to the pre-production on

Do any of these men look gay to you? That's the subtext of Tony Scott's macho fantasy Top Gun *(1986), according to Roger Avary and articulated by Tarantino in a cameo role he played in* Sleep With Me *(see chapter 4). Tom Cruise (right) fixes his gaze on instructor Kelly McGillis most heterosexually. (But note the hand-on-hip stance and his buddy's brush moustache.)*

Tony Scott

British-born but Hollywood-based younger brother (now in his early fifties) of *Alien*, *Blade Runner* and *Thelma and Louise* director Ridley, Tony Scott comes from a similar advertising background. His cinema debut was a vampire movie, *The Hunger* (1983), which betrayed his ad-man origins a mile off – all soft-focus filters and cigarette smoke. Less atmospheric but more breastbeatingly mainstream, *Top Gun* (1986) was a US version of a typical *Boys' Own* romp, with Tom Cruise as the most macho fly-boy at the US Navy's advanced fighter training school. Hugely successful, it allowed Scott to command large fees for future work. The movie's fans included Quentin Tarantino and Roger Avary. From here, Scott found himself pegged as an action director, making standard entries in the genre: *Beverley Hills Cop II* (1987) with Eddie Murphy, *Days of Thunder* (1990), with Tom Cruise, and *The Last Boy Scout* (1991), a typically explosive number starring Bruce Willis. More interesting was *Revenge* (1990), a bloody thriller starring Kevin Costner in an uncharacteristically dark role, as an ex-navy fighter pilot out hunting with Anthony Quinn, an ageing gangster whose life he once saved. The vengeance of the title refers to a violent battle of wills begun by Quinn, when he finds Costner is having an affair with his much younger wife. Tarantino acclaims *Revenge* as one of the greatest movies produced in the 1980s (its release being in early 1990).

'After *Top Gun* the movies that I was offered were, for better or worse, what you call hardware action movies,' admits Scott. 'When I first read *True Romance* I thought, "Here's another violent movie," but it wasn't that. What I fell in love with were Quentin's characters – it's an actor-based movie, the first time I've had one of those – so I chased it. *Reservoir Dogs* was much more of a head trip, I found it very disturbing, but *True Romance* is like doing speed for two hours. I think this is my best work to date.'

In 1995 Tony Scott released *Crimson Tide*, an action drama set aboard a submarine, with script doctoring by his friend Tarantino.

Reservoir Dogs. Lustig was paid a lump sum to walk away; the potential of the vibrantly (and violently) zestful script raising the budget from $6.5 million to $25 million. 'He gave me *True Romance*,' claims Hadida, referring to a relationship with Tarantino that sprang initially from considering him as screenwriter on an adaptation of a French movie. 'I gave one of the scripts to Gregory [Cascante, of August Entertainment], who had already received this script before. I said, "Please read it, and when I come back to Paris, let me know whether you like this guy or not."'

Cascante tells it another way: 'I said to Sammy: "I've found the most exceptional script that I've read in years. Do you have X number of dollars to option this property?" He said, "Tell me the story."' Cascante then synopsised the screenplay over the transatlantic wire to Hadida at his business base in France. 'I said, "Look, why don't I send you the script? Then you can decide." He said: "No, I don't have to read the script. Buy it."'

Over the months that followed, it's unlikely either deal-maker would be so keen to take credit for acquiring the property, as the movie failed to turn a profit at the US box office. (As with *Dogs*, it proved more popular in Britain, though it made good money on video, and it never came close to the low-budget/tidy profit equation of Tarantino's debut.)

The situation changed once more when Tarantino went to a Hollywood party also attended by director Tony Scott and his partner Bill Unger. 'Quentin told me he was a long-standing fan of Tony Scott's,' says Unger. Tarantino impressed him as 'an aficionado about all the little details, big and mundane, about the history of making movies'. He also asked Unger if he'd read any of his screenplays, stating 'he would love it if Tony and I became involved in anything he did'. Keeping the movie debutant's words in mind, Unger says, 'I heard further details about how *Reservoir Dogs* was going, and the cast it was going with, and I felt this was real because of the fact that Harvey Keitel had become attached to the project as a sort of mentor. I knew Harvey and I knew that he was serious about his work.'

'I'd met Tony through a mutual friend and I was a big fan of his work,' remembers Tarantino. 'I'd just gotten *Dogs* off the ground and he had heard who my cast was, so I sent him *True Romance* to read, even though somebody else had it at the time. He said, "I wish there was something we could do about it." And I said, "Take it away from the other guy, I want you to do it."'

So Tarantino's fable of pop-culture-kids-on-the-run was placed in safe, mainstream hands. Before pre-production, Bill Unger asked the nascent wunderkind, 'Look Quentin, would you be interested in doing this as a follow-up to *Reservoir Dogs*?' But he declined to nurture his first-born on the way to the screen, stating: 'I wrote all three [*Romance, Killers, Dogs*] to be my first film and then I made my first film. It's like an old girlfriend, it has a shelf life. And anyway, it was exciting, the idea of seeing my world through Tony's eyes.'

At the point that Tony Scott was climbing aboard, Gregory Cascante was trying to raise part of the budget via the intended distributors, Miramax, who would make a modest hit of *Dogs*. 'Now we have a $25-million movie,' said Cascante. 'Are you in?

And they said, "Oh shit, that's not easy for us." They went around and did their thing and came back to us and said, "No we can't." Miramax, who had come on board promising half of the production cost when the movie was budgeted at just over the $6 million mark, were given a one-off compensation payment and removed from the project, although company head Harvey Weinstein and his brother, Bob, were given a credit on the film as executive producers. Harvey Weinstein claims that when Scott became involved, 'He had an ambition for the project that involved a much higher budget. We didn't want to stand in Tony Scott's way. And so we received a very generous financial package. We saw the film in Cannes and are very proud of it.'

As Miramax bowed out, Morgan Creek offered a guaranteed lump sum upon delivery of the completed print, in return for distribution rights for the USA and Great Britain. Their letter of credit required a completed screenplay, a set budget, final cut for the director, and the top-line cast that was by now being finalised. By early 1993, Hadida and Cascante had negotiated with the French Banque Paribas to provide the movie's entire production costs, their criteria being the involvement of Tony Scott and Christian Slater as the male lead.

In a bar in downtown Detroit a young man tries to pick up an older woman. Amusing at first – with talk of his demi-god, Elvis Presley – he strikes out by inviting her to a late-night kung fu triple bill. Having failed, he's at the cinema on his own and gets talking to a striking young blonde girl who sits next to him. Afterwards, they go for pie and coffee. During their conversation we hear that it's the boy's (Clarence's) birthday, and the girl (Alabama) gives him a list of her favourite things. They hit it off with a vengeance, so Clarence invites her to look around his workplace – Heroes For Sale, a comic book store – then back to his apartment, where they dance to an old record and wind up in bed.

The next morning, Clarence finds a tearful Alabama writing him a confessional letter. She's a hooker and they met by design, the comic store manager hiring her as a birthday gift. Clarence isn't phased, telling her he had more fun than with anyone ever in his life, and that he was relieved to find she didn't have a dick. She's a novice at prostitution and he's only her fourth trick. No matter what the circumstance, the romance is true, and they marry immediately.

Cut to two black men and one white – two 'niggers' and one wannabe-nigger, a cracker in stubble and locks. As a large quantity of cocaine is weighed up, all three are locked in a conversation about cunnilingus, one of the blacks cursing white boys for introducing black women to a practice he finds disgusting. The other two break up at his prudery. Drexl, the white nigger, asks him how he would be if Jayne Kennedy wanted him to eat her up. Then, seemingly in rage at being called a 'white boy', he takes out a shotgun and blows both his companions away. He picks up the suitcase full of cocaine and leaves.

Clarence, meanwhile, is perturbed by thoughts of his new young wife as a hooker, and the way she may have been treated by her pimp, Drexl. In a bathroom conversation with his imaginary mentor, the late great Elvis, he's urged to ease his mind by killing the pimp.

Clarence visits Drexl's apartment, where he's watching a blaxploitation movie and

True Romance: she tastes like a peach, he talks like a geek, but together, Clarence Worley (Christian Slater) and Alabama Whitman (Patricia Arquette) are about to take on the world in their Elvis-style pink Cadillac.

eating Chinese food, surrounded by three strung-out 'rock whores'. Clarence offers payment for the loss of Alabama's services: total $0.00. They lock in a bitter fight, Drexl gaining the upper hand with the help of his crony, beating Clarence close to senseless. Drexl takes Clarence's wallet, reads his address and tells his henchman to go bring Alabama back. As they turn their attention, Clarence draws a revolver from his shoe and shoots Drexl in the crotch. He blows the second banana away mercilessly. The hookers are hysterical, Clarence making one of them bring him Alabama's belongings. She pulls out a suitcase from beneath the bed. He shoots the agonised Drexl point blank through the skull and leaves.

Back at his apartment, Clarence reduces Alabama to tears by telling her he's killed Drexl – but she cries only because she's so moved by the lengths he went to for her. She opens the suitcase to find it doesn't contain her clothes, but is filled with cocaine.

On the run, Clarence and Alabama call in on his father, Clifford, a reformed alcoholic and ex-cop, working as a security guard. Clifford is quietly taken with his new daughter-in-law, but bemused at his son – who he hasn't seen for three years – turning up and asking him a favour. Clarence argues how he's never asked anything of him before, and Clifford resolves to glean information from his friends in the police department. Later, he informs them detectives believe Drexl Spivey was offed by rival gangsters, and was involved in a dispute with a big-timer called Blue Lou Boyle. The lovers take off for Hollywood with the cocaine, Clifford refusing any money for helping them.

Meanwhile, in Tinseltown, a young actor, Dick Ritchie, is auditioning for William Shatner's TV comeback, The Return of T. J. Hooker. On the basis of a one-line reading, the casting agent acclaims him a very good actor and hires him.

Back in Detroit, Clifford returns home to be met by a strong-arm band of thugs, led by Vincenzo Coccotti, right-hand man to Blue Lou Boyle. They hold him while Coccotti administers a beating for lying as to Clarence's whereabouts. (His driving licence was recovered from the scene of Drexl's massacre, and neighbours squealed that his car was parked outside Clifford's place.) Coccotti urges Clifford not to lie, claiming that Sicilians are the best liars in the world. Prompted, Clifford seeks to offend by delivering a monologue about how Sicilians are basically niggers, the descendants of Italian women fucked by Moorish invaders. After a cursory burst of laughter, Clifford's story wins the desired result, and Coccotti blows his brains out.

Back in Hollywood, the two lovers burst in on Dick Ritchie, Clarence's struggling actor friend from Detroit. The two old buddies become three old buddies, as any friend of Alabama's husband is a friend of hers. They're also introduced to Floyd, a space cadet who rooms with Dick. Clarence shares the secret of the cocaine, urging Dick to help them find a big-time buyer who'll take $500,000 worth for $200,000 in one cash payment. Dick complains that he's not 'Joe Cocaine', but relents and promises to fix up a meeting with Elliot Blitzer – a colleague from his acting class who works for Lee Donowitz, a big-name producer.

The trio meet Elliot at the Los Angeles City Zoo, where Clarence feeds him a story about a friend in the LAPD who stole the stash. Meanwhile, back at Dick's apartment, a posse of thugs sent by Coccotti try to menace the whereabouts of Clarence and Alabama out of Floyd, but he's so far off the planet he blithely proffers the information anyway.

Clarence makes contact with Lee Donowitz, couching the coke transaction in terms of a deal to distribute Dr Zhivago. Meanwhile, Alabama returns to the Hollywood Holiday Inn and is met by Virgil, the most formidable of Coccotti's thugs. He starts beating her to within an inch of her life, talking her through the process. Before killing her, the sadistic hitman repays her fierce spirit by letting her take one swing at him with a knife. Confident of stopping the blade, he prepares for a forward lunge, but she drops to her knees and stabs him in the foot. Enraged, he throws her through a glass shower door, but she blinds him with shampoo and pushes broken glass into his face. In the final race for the firearms, Alabama wins and blows Virgil away with a sawn-off shotgun. Clarence arrives and whisks his injured wife and the coke away in his car.

Later, while she sleeps, Clarence is tortured by her loyalty (she narrowly missed death rather than give away his whereabouts), and swears, 'I'll cut off my hands and gouge my eyes out before I ever let anything happen to that lady again.'

Out on the freeway, Elliot is pulled in for speeding, screaming at the hooker in the passenger seat to hide his bag of uncut coke down her bra. She refuses and hits him over the head with it, showering him with white powder as the highway cop arrives.

Down at the precinct, Detectives Nicholson and Dimes (that's Nicky Dimes, for anyone who doesn't get the joke first time) sweat Elliot to cooperate on busting the supplier. Terrified of becoming a prison punk, he agrees to wear a wire.

On the way to the meeting with Donowitz, Clarence is overcome with paranoia and holds Elliot at gunpoint in an elevator, threatening to blow his brains out unless he can explain why he feels so nervous. Overheard by the downhearted cops, Elliot breaks down and begs for someone to take him away. Then, to their amazement, Clarence relents and tries to make it up with Elliot.

In the meeting, Clarence gets on like a house on fire with the producer, enthusing about how Donowitz's Vietnam picture, Comin' Home in a Body Bag, was his favourite Oscar-winning movie. The deal seems to be coming together, but, while Clarence is in the *bathroom confessing his nervousness to the imaginary Elvis, the cops burst in. Donowitz's bodyguard refuses to come peacefully, sounding off with an Uzi in his hand. Then a hit squad sent by the mob also bursts in and chaos breaks loose. Elliot identifies himself as an informer, Donowitz throws scalding coffee in his face, Dimes guns Donowitz down. The room erupts into a pandemonium of bullets, and many of the people there are gunned down, including Clarence. Dick causes a distraction by throwing the cache of coke in the air and running into the corridor, but is halted by a police officer; the cop is gunned down by a hood, who takes one look at the pleading Dick – who only wants to live to get to the T. J. Hooker set on Monday – and lets him go. Back inside the living room, both the chief investigating officers are lying dead. Alabama tearfully cradles Clarence's body, one of his eye sockets filled with blood. He gives a murmur and comes groggily to life – the bullet wound is external, obliterating his eye but not entering his skull. They flee with the suitcase of money Donowitz intended to use to finance the cocaine deal.*

In a sentimental fairy-tale ending narrated by Alabama, she and Clarence (now sporting an eyepatch) live happily ever after on a tropical island, with their son, Elvis.

Despite the guns, profanity and constant movie/trash culture references, there's some disagreement among fans as to whether *True Romance* can be seen as a Tarantino movie *per se*. 'Something that Tony added to it – and it's not like a scene that he wrote, it's just something that comes across in the shooting,' reflects the screenwriter himself, apportioning credit rather than blame. 'He added a fairy-tale element to it, that I don't think was as 100% in mine as it was in his.'

'I think it's very sweet and nice that we do end up together,' says Christian Slater, interpreting the fairy-tale element as Roger Avary's happy ending, 'and it's a beautiful sunset... but yeah, in the original script, that's a rap, which made complete sense because they were living such a fast and spontaneous and chaotic and insane life. But this is the movies... and I'm really proud of it.'

Clarence Worley – the world's most clean-cut rockabilly, as endearingly portrayed by Slater (for credits see Appendix) – was an obvious wish-fulfilment fantasy for Tarantino at the time he wrote (or, took over) the *True Romance* script. Gauche, gushingly earnest, gutsy, with a touching faith in himself that others didn't seem to share, here was a kid at the bottom of the ladder who wasn't going to let his dreams get too tarnished. At one point in the script he testifies to his hatred of airports, how living close to one served to rub his nose in his own poverty. 'Me and my wife are minimum wage kids, two hundred thousand is the world,' he claims later in the movie. Both are sincere Tarantino sentiments, the latter carrying future echoes of a time when $200,000 per script would become a fairly standard fee.

The movie's final triumphant ride into the sunset isn't considered nearly as romantic – at least by the movie's author – as the scenes in the neon-lit comic store, recalling a very different life: 'That whole Video Archives time, even though it's not directly in the movie, it is in the movie. That time is captured perfectly in *True Romance*. It almost takes it to like mythology or something. I mean, not for Joe Shmoe in the street, but it's

Dream girlfriend: the too-good-to-be-true bad girl Alabama.

different for the people at Video Archives. They can't watch the movie without, "Oh wow!", it takes us back. Because the things that Clarence said, they're the things that I and the rest of us said. The conversations that he has are the conversations we had. Our names are throughout the script – Lance [Lawson] is the guy I worked for, he's in the movie.' (As an unseen presence anyway – the store manager who lays on the hooker as a birthday present is referred to as Lance.)

The minor episode where Dick passes his audition for *The Return of T. J. Hooker* seems to be based on Tarantino's own ever-hopeful casting experiences, particularly the solitary time he hit paydirt, as one of 12 Elvis impersonators on an episode of *The Golden Girls*.

Whatever biographical baggage it carries, however, *True Romance* is still a story of boy meets girl. 'When I wrote this I was a guy who hadn't even had a girlfriend,' admits Tarantino. 'I had a lot of dates, but I never had a girlfriend. So Alabama in some ways was kind of a dream girlfriend.'

With the sudden acclaim that came to *Dogs*, Tarantino suddenly found he'd gained both a personal and professional life overnight. Various young women in the industry

were pursued, or seduced, in an almost old-fashioned gentlemanly way. One short-term girlfriend and long-term friend is Allison Anders, director of *Gas Food Lodging* and later contributor to *Four Rooms* (see chapter 7). 'Quentin's a big romantic actually,' she says, 'and I think that couples are very important to him, as is that dynamic – having your girlfriend who's also your pal, like in *True Romance*.'

As well as a dream of the perfect fantasy girl, the *True Romance* script was a lovesick paen to pop culture. Much of Alabama's appeal is based not simply on her sexiness, but on her getting hot over the idea of seeing the X-rated version of the martial arts movie, *The Streetfighter* starring Sonny Chiba, (they've just watched the R-rated version). Alabama isn't just the wet dream of a guy who doesn't get out enough and has no female company – she's a dream-image spawned by the movies: 'She's a 16-calibre kitten, equally equipped for killin' an' lovin'!' enthuses Clarence in the script, embellishing her identity with a movie-trailer talkover. 'She carried a sawed-off shotgun in her purse, a black belt around her waist, and the

Mad Max (1979): George Miller's film is referred to by name in True Romance, *testifying to Tarantino's admiration for the all-action film.*

Below: Clint Eastwood, as the Man With No Name, is about to leave Tuco (Eli Wallach) hanging around at the end of Sergio Leone's The Good, The Bad and The Ugly *(1966).*

white-hot fire of hate in her eyes! Alabama Whitman is Pam Grier! Pray for forgiveness. Rated R... for Ruthless Revenge!' In referring to Pam Grier not only is Tarantino paying tribute to this blaxploitation goddess, he's predetermining the actions of his cutesy-pie fantasy girl. She just has to become a killer.

As soon as Tarantino grabbed the reins from Avary, he layered the script with overt references to the things he loved – movies, Elvis, kung fu, comic books, fast food, and more movies. In the scene when he tries to forge a bond with Lee Donowitz, the producer with whom he's striking a coke deal, the Clarence character – basically a mouthpiece for Tarantino – tells him how he values his Vietnam epic, *Comin' Home in a Body Bag*: 'After *Apocalypse Now* I think it's the best Vietnam movie ever... It was the first movie with balls to win a lot of Oscars since *The Deer Hunter*.' Cue the now-celebrated (or derided) tirade against Academy-approved films – 'safe, geriatric coffee-table dog shit' – with a sneer in the direction of Merchant-Ivory, as opposed to honest, ballsy movies – *Mad Max*, *The Good, The Bad and The Ugly*, *Rio Bravo* and *Rumblefish* are the Tarantino favourites namechecked in the script, but there could have been dozens of others.

'I love movies, I love TV shows, I love breakfast cereal,' says Tarantino. 'I grew up with that, it's like one hundred per cent my consciousness.' By now, his likes – and to a smaller extent, his dislikes – have passed into the popular consciousness. *True Romance*, however, was where the auteur-in-the-making first nailed his colours to the mast.

The movie opens with Clarence (Christian Slater) worshipping Elvis: 'I saw *Jailhouse Rock* and I wanted to be that hillbilly.' (This opening eulogy, which has our hero telling the woman he's trying to pick up that 'I'm no fag, but... I'd fuck Elvis,' is lifted from *My Best Friend's Birthday*, Tarantino's abandoned amateur production with Craig Hamann and Rand Vossler.) Clarence and Alabama even flee Detroit for LA in a pink Cadillac, the ultimate white trash luxury, as owned by The King himself.

'That's one of the things I get a big kick out of,' says the trash culture wunderkind, in acknowledgement of his Elvis obsession, and the casting of Val Kilmer in the role of the Memphis Flash himself, acting as Clarence's imaginary guardian angel. (In the cast list he's simply referred to as 'Mentor', to prevent the Presley estate muscling in for any kind of royalties deal. Kilmer gives a creditable blast of 'Heartbreak Hotel' on the soundtrack, however.) 'As opposed to *Play It Again Sam*, with Bogart telling Woody Allen how to get in with the chicks, Elvis is just saying "Kill that guy."'

'Val spent eight hours in make-up trying to look like Elvis, and he looked brilliant,' Scott commented. 'Originally I showed it so I could see his face, but there's only one person who looks like Elvis, and that's Presley, and so I redesigned it. But Val is brilliant, he became Elvis three months before we did it and he only had two days' work. I'd talk to him on the phone and it's like [curl-lipped drawl] "Hey." He only plays dead rock and rollers now.' (Scott was refering to Kilmer's earlier role as Jim Morrison in *The Doors*, but the actor has ventured further into pop-culture icon territory with the title role of *Batman Forever*.)

Alexandre Rockwell – director of *In the Soup*, which previewed at the Sundance Festival the same time as *Reservoir Dogs* (January '92), more recently a contributor to Four Rooms – tells a story of how he visited a New York restaurant called Two Boots with Tarantino: 'We ate this peanut cream pie. He said, "Ya know something Alex?" "What?" "If Elvis Presley ate peanuts and came, this is what it would taste like." The pie came out of my nose when he said that. It was his way of saying it's the best pie he's ever eaten. Immediately, we ordered another piece. Somehow, Elvis was never better.'

Despite Clarence's Elvis/rockabilly fetish, Scott filled the soundtrack with a catholic selection of styles spanning four decades – from Burl Ives and 'Chantilly Lace' by The Big Bopper (Clarence greets his buddy Dick with the cheesy 'He-llo Baby!' that the Bopper kick-starts the song with), to a painfully slick modern synth-rock ballad and Chris Isaak's update on the Roy Orbison brand of melancholic romance. (The ending of the original script called for Alabama to flee the scene of Clarence's death, making off with the money and his favourite comic, till reduced to tears by the poignant kitsch of Leapy Lee's 'Little Arrows'.)

Even the decidedly non-trashy titles music, by Hans Zimmer, is a further pop-culture echo, a version of the rhythmically Satiesque theme from *Badlands*, as culled from *Lakme* by Leo Delibes. Scott had clearly decided not to disguise what he considered the

Terence Malick's Badlands *(1974), a melancholic evocation of aimless young white trash turned to murder, has had a lasting effect, not least on Tarantino. Its main characters, Kit Carruthers (Martin Sheen) and his under-age girlfriend Holly (Sissy Spacek), are simple-minded dreamers who go on a killing spree across the Midwest.* True Romance *shares both its theme of bad boy/bad girl on the run and its theme music. Malick's movie was based on the true case of Charlie Starkweather and Caril Fugate, who were only 17 and 14 respectively when they set off on a killing spree in 1958.*

movie's nearest antecedents, even though the character of Clarence is a million miles from Badland's vacuously ruthless Kit Carruthers, himself based on real-life spree killer Charlie Starkweather.

More movie esoterica: in Tarantino's original script, one of the Italian-American goons who menace Clifford is named 'Dario', after Dario Argento, his favourite Italian horror director. At another point (in the script, rather than the movie), Clarence tries to break through Alabama's wilful sense of mystery by asking, 'What're you tryin' to be? The Phantom Lady?' *Phantom Lady*, a 1940s *noir*, was adapted from a story by Cornell Woolrich, one of the darker pulp crime writers, and an influence on *Pulp Fiction*.

Sonny Chiba

Clarence lucks out with the barroom blonde he's trying to pull pre-credits by inviting her to a 'Sonny Chiba triple bill' – *The Streetfighter*, *Return of the Streetfighter* and *Sister Streetfighter* – and an excerpt from one of the martial arts star's movies occupies the screen pre-credits, as Alabama makes up to Clarence in the movie house. (In the original script, the newlyweds watch a martial arts movie on TV which appears to be a hybrid of *The One-Armed Boxer* and *Masters of the Flying Guillotine*, two 1970s epics with kung fu star Jimmy Wang Yu which live up to the grotesquerie of their titles.) Chiba, star of the *Shadow Warriors* TV series, was a hero of the old gang at Video Archives. He'd eventually turn up on the set of *Pulp Fiction*, to watch Samuel Jackson quoting from *Ezekiel* before icing a hit. Despite its evocation of Southern Gothic, Tarantino claims this is close to a stand-by of the Chiba TV character, who would always give a speech on morality before slaughtering an enemy.

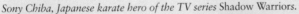

Sony Chiba, Japanese karate hero of the TV series Shadow Warriors.

When Clarence enters Drexl's place, trying to steel his nerves and kill the bastard, the lowlife is watching *The Mack*, a blaxploitation movie for which the white boy effortlessly reels off the main credits.

Most obviously, in the middle of the cocaine deal, Clarence jumps in his car and says to himself, 'We now return you to *Bullitt* in progress,' which needs little explanation. Most obscurely, when Clarence is trying to negotiate the drug deal with Donowitz, he tells him, 'you're just gonna have to come to terms with your Fear and Desire'. The script capitalises the words, forming a reference to *Fear and Desire*, Stanley Kubrick's first independent feature, set in an unspecified war zone.

Even Drexl is a movie buff. When Clarence tries to come on hard, he jokingly compares the white boy to Charles Bronson, specifically to a forgotten 1974 thriller called *Mr Majestyk*, which stars the stone-faced one as a melon farmer defending his livelihood against the mob. (The movie was scripted by Elmore Leonard, now a literary superstar in his own right, and Tarantino's favourite living crime fiction writer.)

In the original script, Alabama complains how Drexl enticed her via a fantasy image of herself. She wanted to be one of the hookers who 'drive Porsches, live in condos, have stockbrokers, carry beepers, you know, like Nancy Allen in

Geek with a gun: Clarence plays it just like he's seen it in the movies.

Dressed to Kill'. In Tarantino's world, everyone's a movie geek, remembering titles, cast and credits. However, many of the obsessive film references were cut by Scott when he brought the script to the screen.

Critics of the movie's supposed nihilism couldn't see past the violence and appreciate its celebratory tone. (Even the violence is in itself a celebration, not of real-life brutality, but, as Patricia Arquette says, of America's love affair with violent screen images.) 1960s kids' TV shows are saluted in the dialogue, from Hanna Barbera cartoons – 'This should cover it, Auggie-Doggy'; 'Okie-dokie, Doggy-daddy'; 'You did it Quickdraw [McGraw], I'm so proud of you' – to superhero shows – 'Riddle me this, Batman'.

Tarantino's anti-elitist ethic is seen applying to comic books, the ultimate trash collectable, in the Heroes For Sale sequence, as he makes Alabama a gift of his favourite comic book, *Sgt Fury & His Howling Commandoes*: 'One of the coolest series known to man. They're completely worthless. You can get number one for about four bucks.' In the original script we catch a further glimpse of the child-like (even childish) artefacts that brighten up his world. Clarence refers to the other superhero ephemera they sell in the store: '*Man From U.N.C.L.E.* lunch boxes. Green Hornet board games. Shit like that.' Shit like that plays a big role in Tarantino's social life, drinking into the small hours with his friends while playing TV and movie-related board games. (This was how he befriended John Travolta, icon to the children of the 70s – see chapter 5.) Later, when he's holding Elliot Blitzer at gunpoint, to determine just how straight up the deal is,

Breathless *(1983): 'Jim McBride's version of* Breathless *was an extremely influential movie for me... here's a movie that's indulging completely in all of my obsessions: comic books...rockabilly music...and also in the form of movies. Not that the characters sit around and talk about movies all the time, but with the use of cheap process shots going on behind them throughout the whole film.'*

Clarence brazens out the words: 'Like Nick Carter used to say, if I'm wrong I'll apologize.' Carter was the nearest literary equivalent to TV shows like *The Man From U.N.C.L.E.*, but with more liberal doses of sex and violence. Largely forgotten now, each book in the series was written by hacks under the pseudonym Nick Carter, as if they themselves were the play-rough agent.

Even junk food is paid sincere tribute. Clarence sends Alabama out to buy fried chicken and beer, but is disappointed to find the necessary outlets aren't open at 9am. When Clarence goes to a Mexican burger bar to buy both of them some food, he asks for the biggest, fattest hamburger: a double chili cheese. Naturally, sharing all Tarantino's tastes (and his appetite), he orders two of them, plus two large portions of chili fries, one combination burrito and two large Diet Cokes (gotta watch those calories). The line, 'Eat something – you'll feel better,' when Clarence instructs Alabama to take some fries after fessing up to the killing of her pimp, is a junk food anticlimax first used in John McNaughton's account of a mass murderer, *Henry: Portrait of a Serial Killer* where Henry tells his nervous sidekick, Otis, to take a handful of french fries after strangling two hookers and dumping them in a skip.

The major appeal of the movie to its cultish, but by no means tiny audience (enough to hand over $20,000,000 at the US box office, but not enough to make it turn a profit) was much the same as Alabama's appeal to Clarence. 'You like all the same stuff that I do!' he gushes to her at one point, though she has to fess up and tell him she was lying about *The Partridge Family*. (Tarantino's own affections for this middle-American-family-cum-manufactured-pop-group originate way back, in kids' TV culture – see his tribute to *The Partridge Family* as a life-saver in *My Best Friend's Birthday*, chapter 1).

When Alabama tells Clarence that the finer things in life for her include 'Mickey Rourke, Elvis's voice, good kung fu, pot, and a tasty piece of pie,' it's not just Tarantino speaking aloud his wish-fulfilment fantasy of the perfect girlfriend; he's reaching out to his audience for the first time, touching the hands of thousands of trash consumers for whom such items also constitute the good things of life.

Despite his dislike of Oliver Stone's later revision of *Natural Born Killers*, Tarantino remained uncharacteristically tolerant of liberties taken with this first script: '*True Romance* wasn't written in a linear fashion originally. It started off with the same first scene of Clarence talking about Elvis, then the next scene was Drexl killing all his cronies and the third scene was Clarence and Alabama at Clarence's father's house. And then you learn how he got what he got. Tony made it all linear and it worked that way.

'If you break it into three acts, the structure they all worked under was: in the first act the audience really doesn't know what's going on, they're just getting to know the characters. The characters have far more information than the audience has. By the second act you start catching up and get even with the characters, and then in the third act you now know far more than the characters know, you're way ahead of the characters. That was the structure *True Romance* was based on and you can totally apply that to *Reservoir Dogs*.'

'Tony Scott actually started putting it together that way in the editing room, but he said it didn't work for him. I guess what I'm always trying to do is use these structures that I see in novels and apply them to cinema.'

Belying the idea that his trashy sensibilities are composed of nothing but movie memories, Tarantino would eventually take his most audacious – and most successful – structural liberties with *Pulp Fiction*.

Meanwhile, most debate centred – as it would for all Tarantino's work – on the movie's violence, and whether or not it could be termed gratuitous. Coming on like Mr Blonde, who doesn't know what 'gratuitous' means, Christian Slater saw through the bloody trappings surrounding his character: 'I thought he [Clarence] was sweet and sensitive. He loved the movies. He always wanted to be a part of them in some way, and Alabama opened the door and it gave him the opportunity to be the hero. Somebody said to me it sorta picks up where *Taxi Driver* left off.'

By the time the movie was delivered to Morgan Creek in the first week of July 1993, it had been through a baptism of fire with the US ratings board, the Motion Picture Association of America (MPAA). Over a three-week wrangle, the filmmakers had been made to agree to the re-edit of several scenes in order to gain an 'R'-rating – rather than the feared 'NC-17', which allows no-one in below that age, and cuts the box office considerably. Tony Scott was forced to compromise and edit two different versions – the 'domestic cut' and the 'foreign version'. (Ironically, the print distributed in the censorious

Tarantino (left) in the opening credits sequence of Reservoir Dogs.

'Let's go to work': British Reservoir Dogs *poster*

Nice Guy Eddie (Chris Penn) and Mr Blonde (Michael Madsen) from Reservoir Dogs.

Zed (Eric Stolz), still suffering the effects of his introduction to heroin, during a bank raid in Killing Zoe, the debut feature by Tarantino's former collaborator Roger Avary.

Sultry femme fatale Uma Thurman gives a come-on to the punters in the Pulp Fiction *poster.*

Mia (Uma Thurman) and Vincent (John Travolta) get cosy in the mocked-up 50s car body that serves as a table in Jack Rabbit Slim's.

A rare moment of tenderness in Pulp Fiction: *fugitive boxer Butch (Bruce Willis) makes love to Fabienne (Maria de Madeiros).*

In one of the framing scenes of Pulp Fiction, *Pumpkin and Honey Bunny hit on a great spot for a hold-up: the coffee house where they are having breakfast.*

Lance (Eric Stoltz) tries to prevent Vincent bringing the OD'd Mia round for a cardiac jumpstart. In the next cut, the car skids to a halt on his front lawn.

Murder boosts ratings: Wayne Gale (Robert Downey, Jr.), creator of the American Maniacs *TV show, tells the imprisoned Mickey he's going to make him a star. (From* Natural Born Killers*)*

Mickey and Mallory pledge themselves to each other in a do-it-yourself wedding.

'Suck on this!' Robert De Niro glories in the prospect of violent retribution in Taxi Driver, *Martin Scorsese's classic descent into urban hell. Travis Bickle (Robert De Niro) is about to turn his festering psychosis loose on the occupants of a seedy brothel that exploits child whore Iris (Jodie Foster). Tarantino, who numbers* Taxi Driver *among his All-Time Top Three, sees* True Romance *as the latest in a loose lineage trailing from the film: 'What I like about what Clarence does is that he makes a choice to go in there and kill this pimp, and it's funny because it's kind of psychotic... he's seen a million movies about pimps beating up whores and he remembers the scene in* Taxi Driver *when Harvey Keitel is talking about Jodie Foster, describing it in all these real graphic terms. He can imagine this pimp, who he's never even met, talking about his gal, his lady love, like that, so he has to go over there and execute him.'*

UK falls somewhere between the two, the video even being advertised as 'The Uncut Version'.) The MPAA were also bothered by the sequence where Clarence wipes out Drexl. 'They objected more to the tone of Christian's performance than the amount of blood,' complains Scott. The fresh-faced killer – who has also been beaten within a short distance of his life – apparently proved a little too triumphant. 'The violence is integral to these characters. And as a director, I feel those moments are [now] unfulfilled and never quite reach their peak.'

'It's heartbreaking,' elaborates Scott, who would have been in violation of his contract if he had made an unlucrative 'NC17' movie. 'Each year the ratings board gets tougher, especially in terms of violence. They don't like movies like this.

'The major change for me is that Patricia [Arquette, as Alabama] originally got to shoot Chris Penn [as Officer Dimes], which enabled her to be instrumental in terms of their running off with the money. Now it's an incidental character, the Italian lying on the floor, who gets to do the shooting.

'What made it worse was that it was a woman. That's what they said: "A woman shooting a policeman, that makes it even worse..."'

The intensity of Alabama's revenge on Virgil, the hitman, also caused a wringing of hands. 'There's a scene in which Patricia, who has been beaten and thrown through a shower stall, eventually exhausts herself in every possible way in terms of beating him. We had to cut a section where, after she unloads the gun on the thug, she beats him with the barrel – which I thought was justified because it was not gratuitous. It was the true revenge of the character.' Rather than simply blowing the sadistic goon away, Scott had her follow the original script and erupt in a frenzy of vengefulness, filling various parts of his body with bullets before battering his already bloody head with the gun butt.

Here's to success: minimum-wage kids Clarence and Alabama live it up in a Hollywood hotel, unaware that sadistic hitman Virgil is just around the corner.

Revenge, it seems, is a man's business, and we can't have little girls getting bloodthirsty, no matter how they've been treated. Fortunately, Scott's alternative take – with Virgil's head blasted away after Alabama almost seems to give up the ghost, collapsing to the floor and praying for strength – loses little of its momentum. With the action coming close on the heels of her protracted beating and near murder, there's no doubt who the audience is rooting for. Still, letting the poor little thang receive so much hurt, but only give a limited amount in return, makes censorship a more dubious nonsense than ever.

'I wanted Alabama to get to a point where – although she wasn't enjoying being beaten by Virgil – it would be emotionally painful to her to kill him,' says Patricia Arquette. 'As Alabama, I know one of us is going to end up dead, and it's not gonna be me. I wondered about Alabama's thought process, walking into a room and seeing someone with a gun, and I just figured she felt like, Well, I can't run, or you'll shoot me. I can't scream, or you'll shoot me. But what I can do is freak you out. She knows Clarence is coming back, so even if Virgil is hitting her, the more time he spends on her, the better chance she has of being saved.'

Virgil even takes a little time out to explain to Alabama what it's like to be a hitman, and to make your first kill: 'Now, the first guy you kill is always the hardest. I don't care if you're the Boston Strangler or Wyatt Earp. You can bet that Texas boy, Charles Whitman, the fella who took all them guys from the tower... that first little black dot that he took a bead on was the bitch of the bunch.' As quoted *verbatim* from the original screenplay, it emphasises Tarantino's total assimilation of American violence-culture – from the Wild West to serial killers. It also makes the act of taking a life seem totally alien to a good-natured little fizzbomb like Alabama, crooked as she may be.

'It's as if he's saying to Alabama, when he finally realises she is going to kill him,' reflects Ms Arquette, 'okay, you're gonna embark on this, now let me explain to you what my experience was at that rite of passage... That's what I love about Quentin Tarantino's writing... When he writes violence, it is violent. It's not some phoney violence that's acceptable. Violence shakes you up. Violence isn't pretty.'

'[Violence] isn't about lowering people from helicopters onto speeding trains,' says Tarantino, 'or about terrorists hijacking something or other. Real-life violence is, you're in a restaurant and a man and wife are having an argument and all of a sudden that guy gets so mad at her, he picks up a fork and stabs her in the face. That's really crazy and comic-bookish – but it also happens; that's how real violence comes kicking and screaming into your perspective in real life.'

Paradoxically, Patricia Arquette also states, that 'the movie is as much fantasy as any movie can be. There's the romance between Alabama and Clarence, and then there's the violence. If you've grown up on TV the way I did and the way most people who are Alabama and Clarence's age did, then you grew up with The *Dukes of Hazzard*, Starsky and Hutch, and *Gunsmoke*, where people are dying all the time. It's almost like *True Romance* is about the fantasy America has with violence.'

Her screenwriter implicitly agrees, seeing middle-America and lowlife USA's respective love affairs with TV and violence as separate, but related.

'If you ever saw kids playing, three little kids playing Starsky and Hutch interrogating a prisoner – you'll probably see more real, honest moments happening than you would ever see on that show, because those kids would be so into it. When a kid points his finger at you like it's a gun, he ain't screwing around, that's a gun where he's coming from.'

The dangerous side of Alabama's character is revealed in a line of dialogue in *Reservoir Dogs*, when Joe Cabot asks Mr White what happened to him and Alabama. In Tarantino's universe, which incorporates the original script of *True Romance*, Clarence died and Alabama hooked up with Mr White. Despite the I'm-so-sweet-I-shit-chocolate persona, Alabama Whitman has all the charm and about enough cunning to be the female half of a thieves' partnership.

Cherry-bomb blonde Patricia personified Alabama in a turquoise bra, polka-dot Marilyn blouse and tacky Lolita-style shades. Between *True Romance* and her next notable role, in Tim Burton's *Ed Wood* (Tarantino's favourite movie of 1994), her cutthroat-kitten sexuality gained her a lucrative gig advertising Armani jeans. Who says you can't be violent and sexy at the same time? (Ms Arquette also picked up the movie's pink Cadillac, as a parting gift from the director.)

This girl is alluringly (and knowingly) cute, her sexuality verging on dangerous. A full on-the-mouth kiss she gives her father-in-law, Clifford (Dennis Hopper), carries an almost-incestuous charge. 'I've had directors say to me, "Okay, what we're trying to make the audience believe is this or that." And I say, "That's not my job, buddy. I want people to think." I didn't want to play Alabama with those kind of narrow expectations. She's not the perfect gal. When she kisses Clarence's dad, that's a little questionable. But there's danger in love,' she laughs, with a hint of pride.

Right after the dangerous moment, startled Dad smacks his lips and decides his son is right in saying that she tastes like a peach. 'I tried to get the make-up people to run out and get this kissable lip gloss from the 70s that came in all different tastes, like apple, green apple, and so on. I wanted to put peach on, so after Dennis kissed me he could lick his lips and go, "Oh fuck, she really does taste like it." But we couldn't get any, so Dennis had to use his own sense memory.'

Arquette concurs that, though Alabama is no natural born killer, there's an ambiguity to her character that makes you wonder how much she herself is playing the role of a cute little coquette, wearing a comfortable persona just to make life easier. After all, when she meets Clarence she's working as a hooker, however briefly.

'You're supposed to believe anything you want, but she's not always telling the truth,' Arquette opines. 'For starters, as far as I'm concerned, she doesn't really have that Southern accent, that's an affectation. She decided that was sexy and she's gonna be that Southern Belle.' Much like her creator deciding the myth works better if he's the genius offspring of wild hillbillies.

As with all the incidental details, the movie's minor characters play pivotal parts. The cast has links with Tarantino projects past and future. One of the black coke dealers blown away by the mad dog Milkybar Rasta, Drexl Spivey (Gary Oldman), is played by Samuel L. Jackson. Jackson, who smarted over losing out in the audition for the role of Agent Holdaway in *Dogs*, would later be rewarded with the far more substantial part of Jules in *Pulp Fiction*, for which he received a Best Supporting Actor Academy Award nomination. Meanwhile, the role of Officer Dimes, a considerably bulkier LAPD officer than Freddy Newendyke in *Dogs*, is played by Nice Guy Eddie himself, Chris Penn, looking more corpulent in shirt and tie than in the baggy shell-suit worn previously.

Floyd, the stoned slacker who blithely gives away Clarence and Alabama's location to the mob, is portrayed by Brad Pitt, who one year previously had appeared with Juliette Lewis in *Kalifornia*, another violent road movie. 'You know, Brad has a mystery and a darkness,' says Tony Scott, 'I think it comes from the chequered life he had before. But the bong was my invention,' he adds, referring to how he and Pitt made Floyd a terminally spaced-out dopehead, rather than just a couch potato representing many a Tarantino room-mate. 'There's a guy I go rock climbing with and he has this bong [water pipe], a honey bear jar that you can buy across the counter – he calls his Russ. That was a homage to Russ.'

True Romance often plays likes a series of star cameos, held loosely together by the whimsically murderous love story of Clarence and Alabama. This is largely due to the high-calibre names who lined up for five-minute roles, but, as Tarantino explains, the intent was always there in the script: 'Clarence and Alabama keep running into all these people, and when they do, the movie becomes the story of the people they meet. When

Clarence bawls out his old man, Clifford (Dennis Hopper), over giving a little fatherly assistance.

they're with Clarence's father, I treat him as though the whole movie is going to be about him. When Vincenzo Coccotti, the gangster that Christopher Walken plays, comes in, the whole movie could be about him. The same thing with Drexl, the Gary Oldman character. But particularly the father – you just figure he's going to play a central role.'

Many Tarantino-supporting critics have credited (or blamed) Tony Scott for *True Romance*'s golden glow of Hollywood sentimentality, while insisting their man was responsible for any remaining roughneck elements. Much as Clifford's 'Sicilians are really niggers' speech was as un-PC and as provocatively skilful in its handling of everyday bigotry as Vic and Eddie's 'nigger semen' bullshit in *Dogs*, Tarantino credits Scott for the way it played: 'People think you shoot a lot of different angles just because you're doing action. That's true, but the thing is, it's also a big performance thing.' The newly arrived movie geek was duly impressed by how the action director turned one of his by-now trademark scenes of intense dialogue into something more cinematic. 'When you look at the way Tony Scott did the Christopher Walken-Dennis Hopper scene in *True Romance*, a million different angles, but it's all cut to a performance rhythm… His whole style is to have a cut every 15 seconds.'

Still, the visceral impact is contained in the script, and the context in which it makes wry, dramatic use of the white liberal's most verboten noun. Any concerned viewers – usually white – who can't stomach the use of the N-word in *True Romance* are inclined to baulk at Gary Oldman playing a ghetto-accented 'wannabe-nigger', jeering at Clarence that if he wanted to fight him he ought to have come on 'White Boys' Day'. Such sanctimonious souls presumably never encountered Drexl's counterparts in real life, comical neither-fish-nor-fowl characters who provide a laugh for all racial groups. It's also easy to overlook Alabama's dismissal of the supposed roots of his affected blackness – 'He says his mother was Apache, but I suspect he's lying.' It sounds almost as if Tarantino is having a quiet laugh at the biographical myth constructed around him of a 'part-Cherokee' racial origin.

'I actually think "nigger' may be the most taboo word in the English language. Words should not have that much power,' Tarantino protests, unconsciously recalling 'sick' comedian Lenny Bruce, and his call to neutralise the word's offence by using it matter-of-factly. 'Any time you have a word that does, you should strip the power away. It's nit-picking to be offended just by the use of the word... that's a very limited view and it doesn't really affect me, but I love that speech, it's really funny. It was actually a black guy who told me that whole story.'

'Yeah, I was more worried about the Sicilians,' laughs Dennis Hopper, deliverer of the monologue. 'I figured that it would probably rub a few people the wrong way, but that's okay, and anyway, as a screen actor you don't have speeches in movies any more. This is a speech. I'm a great admirer of Tarantino's writing.'

'If I were to write a script and sell it now,' says the flamekeeper of modern-day Americana, 'I would make the provision that they wouldn't change anything. I can do that now, but at the time I was selling *True Romance* to get the money to make *Reservoir Dogs* it never occurred to me it would get changed. At first, I was really distraught about it; in fact, I was talking about taking my name off the film. I had a lot of faith in Tony Scott – I'm a big fan of his work, especially *Revenge* – but where I was coming from, you just couldn't change my ending.

'Anyway, we got together and talked about it, and Tony said that he wanted to change the ending in particular, not for commercial reasons, but because he really liked these kids and he wanted to see them get away. He said, "Quentin, I'm going to defer to you. I'm going to shoot both endings, then I'm going to look at them, and then decide which one I want to go with."'

The sweetly amoral fairy-tale ending, with Clarence and Alabama getting clean away with their ill-gotten gains and living happily ever after, won hands down.

That very same sentimental ending was the one already written to order by Roger Avary at Margolis' behest. When the film was premiered, Avary claimed to hear many of his own lines from the original collaborative script. At the time of *True Romance's* release, he had been paid less than one thousand dollars for his rewrite of the ending, receiving no screen credit at all for his contributions to the screenplay. Of two young screenwriters coming from the same nowhere existence, from the same obsessive fan base, only one had learned to play the Hollywood game. This was no TV board game – it was played for keeps.

CHAPTER 4

Intermission and trailers

In the 18-month interim between the releases of *Reservoir Dogs* and *Pulp Fiction*, Quentin Tarantino became a *bona fide* media personality – particularly in Britain. Appetites were also whetted by the well-received 'unofficial' second Tarantino movie, *True Romance*, and a sense of anticipation infected everyone who couldn't wait to see how he'd try to top the first, or who just wanted to see him fall flat on his face.

By the time of *Pulp Fiction*'s British release, in October 1994, Tarantino was something of a cultural commentator – at least to those who liked their movie entertainment direct and visceral, but without any cerebral handicaps. BBC TV commemorated the occasion with the *Hollywood's Boy Wonder* documentary for *Arena*; on the ITV network, he was interviewed for Carlton's *Big City* show, with two nubile young women in boxing gloves pounding a punch-bag in the background.

In the *Big City* he talked about *Pulp Fiction*'s playful treatment of the action genre: 'Sure, you don't expect someone like Arnold Schwarzenegger to be sitting in a car and all of a sudden to accidentally let off a few rounds from his Uzi, chugga-chugga-chugga-chugga, killing five people at a bus stop, but it happens in my movies because I like taking genre characters and putting them in real-life situations for comic effect you know so like...'

The first interview was suddenly aborted by the news that the camera was no longer working.

'What, you mean I've burned out the batteries?' queried Tarantino, amused. 'Hey, cool.'

Quentin Tarantino had first met the world head-on during a *Reservoir Dogs* promotional tour that had lasted a whole year. While the 'world tour' contributed greatly to *Dogs*' international success, it's fair to say that its creator appeared to many like some composite Beavis and Butthead of the movie world. It wasn't just his fondness for their favourite adjective either. Garrulous and effusive (without the benefit of what the intelligentsia would consider articulacy), obsessively in love with movies and the whole realm of pop culture they inhabit, gesticulating wildly as he spoke; he played the role of the movie geek to the hilt, looking too consumed by his obsessions to give headroom to decisions about how to dress. Promotional t-shirt and jeans was the uniform, with wild and crazy hair for a wild and crazy guy.

This time around, he'd got wise; to the European audience, Tarantino's movies – and even some of his characters – were the very epitome of cool. As if to remain faithful to his creations, he'd taken a little of their style on board: flyaway hair cut short and brushed back into a nascent quiff; shirt and casual suit, even a dark number that wouldn't look out of place on a Reservoir Dog; in full photographic mode, he donned a white dinner jacket and a wide-collared Vegas shirt. The man was living up to his art.

But the motormouth remained the same, at least in his effusiveness and sheer naked joy in marrying anecdotes to movie trivia. If the stories were followed through to their conclusion without so much digression, if the opinions and eulogies to favourite movies – whether critically revered, despised or downright ignored – flowed just as fast but with more discipline, it was because he didn't have to fight to be heard any more. There were people out there hanging on to his every word.

Leaving the USA for the first time had been a belated growing-up experience. Film festivals were the pretext for travelling, but Europe had provided stimulation for Tarantino's next all-important directorial project. In Amsterdam he spent time openly relaxing and dreaming in a hash bar called Betty Boop; in Paris he sampled the civilised pleasure of cold beer in fast food restaurants, uncommon in the puritanically regulated USA – experiences that appear in *Pulp Fiction*'s opening dialogue. At one point, he joked to friends that he should write a book entitled A Young Filmmaker's Guide to Getting Laid at Film Festivals. With tongue imbedded only partly in cheek, he boasted of luring 'Stockholm babes' to the magazine racks in airports; one look at their man on several magazine covers, and he'd mark up another notch on the headboard of his hotel bed.

By the time of returning to the US, Tarantino was not only looking at his country through new eyes, he could see the seemingly endless possibilities opening up in his own life. In a mixed state of euphoria and hyper-intensity, his glance at the bigger picture had already worked its way into his next, more panoramic script.

On 28 January 1995 the National Film Theatre in London hosted a special screening of the realisation of that script, preceded by a three-week season and followed by a further week of some of Tarantino's favourite movies. For *Pulp Fiction* and the interview Tarantino gave afterwards the main NFT auditorium was packed to full capacity with 450 fans; the smaller screening room next door linked by a video relay took another 350. Ticket applications for the night had totalled more than 4,000, leaving 80 per cent of the fans disappointed.

During the round of interviews that accompanied the season, cinema journalist Tom Shone suggested to Tarantino that he shares the 'American Triumphalist' tone of right-wing satirist and liberal-baiter P. J. O'Rourke. His interviewee was only too happy to agree, painting this picture of himself as the most consumerist of consumers:

'I get a kick out of the fact that you can buy Coca-Cola all over the world, that you can get Dunkin' Donuts all over the world, eat McDonald's all over the world. I never feel I know a country until I've eaten at their McDonald's. Now, I'm joking, but it's also kinda true. McDonald's isn't culture, but there's something kinda sweet, cool that everywhere you go they know what a Big Mac is. It's little things like that, like Coca-Cola and Big Macs and Madonna and Elvis Presley and Muhammad Ali and Kevin Costner, that make us part of a world, whether we like it or not.'

Tarantino's favourite moviemakers and movies

Howard Hawks: 'I like the subtext of friendship and camaraderie.'

Like journalists Cary Grant and Rosalind Russell in His Girl Friday, *Howard Hawks' 1940 gender-change remake of Ben Hecht's* The Front Page, *Tarantino believes that you can't beat a good story. He credits the zest and verve of the movie's dialogue as an influence, using its overlapping speech-style in the exchange between Pumpkin and Honey Bunny in the opening of* Pulp Fiction *(see chapter 5).*

Brian De Palma: 'De Palma was probably like the first working director of his generation that I got into. It's exciting when you love someone who's currently making movies and you're waiting for their new one. I read every review of De Palma's, every interview, and I collected them.'

Martin Scorsese: 'I make a point of not talking about Scorsese any more because everyone else does when they talk about me. I think it's unfair, but I understand it completely. I mean, here's the deal: Scorsese deals in the gangster genre; so do I. Scorsese makes violent films; so do I. Scorsese moves the camera around a lot; so do I. Scorsese uses Harvey Keitel, I use Harvey Keitel. Scorsese is a big film buff, I'm a big film buff. I mean, so what? One guy even said, you use the f-word a lot: did you get that from Scorsese? Occasionally, they'll make a good critical analogy but mostly it's all too pat and easy. What matters is that the end result is so different.'

Jean-Luc Godard: 'That's one aspect of Godard that I found very liberating – movies commenting on themselves, movies and movie history. To me, Godard did to movies what Bob Dylan did to music: they both revolutionized their forms. There were always movie buffs who understood film and film convention, but now, with the advent of video, almost everybody has become a film expert even though they don't know it.'

Above: Breathless *(A Bout de Souffle; 1959). Before his filmmaking career imploded in his obsessive quest to reject the narrative language of la bourgeoisie, Jean-Luc Godard made stylistically stunning, occasionally disturbing use of the genre movie.* Breathless *is dedicated to Monogram Pictures, a US poverty-row company who produced a slew of grainy thrillers which never made it above 'B'-status on a double bill.*

Top right: Poster for Roger Corman's Attack of the Crab Monsters *(1956). For the 'King of the Quickies', specialising in every exploitable genre but with interesting quirks (female gunslingers, beatnik murderers), ten days was a long shoot, three or four nearer the average. Corman produced the early work of directors as diverse as Francis Ford Coppola (*Dementia 13*), Peter Bogdanovich (*Targets*), Monte Hellman (*The Beast from the Haunted Cave*), Martin Scorsese (*Boxcar Bertha*) and Jonathan Demme (*Caged Heat*). Tarantino has jokingly compared* Reservoir Dogs *to a 50s Corman monster movie, in that there's very little violence on screen, but the characters spend most of the movie talking about it.*

Above right: Shock Corridor *(1964), probably Samuel Fuller's most influential movie, set in a mental hospital, and containing some of the most successful hallucinatory footage in the cinema.*

Samuel Fuller: Any hardboiled movie fan can see the debt (in *Reservoir Dogs*) to one of the movie geek's three major self-proclaimed influences: Samuel Fuller, the cigar-chomping veteran director and former newshound. Fuller's violence was always intoxicating, tracking the action in long shot while keeping the punching and shooting bodies in central perspective, following until some fell dead or one punched the fuck out of the other. *Reservoir Dogs* advanced the approach a little further, keeping up the fast pace while bringing a greater immediacy and realism to the violence. Martin Scorsese, also a Fuller fan, has also used the technique to great effect: the poolhall fight in *Mean Streets*, the intensely bloody bordello massacre at the climax of *Taxi Driver*).

Walter Hill: 'The big difference between what I'm doing and what Hill did is that he plays his tough-guy existentialism straight, and I don't have the guts to go all the way... I want to have a little bit of fun with it. I like tough-guy existentialsim with a little bit of a twist.'

On the set of Walter Hill's The Driver *(1978).*

Abel Ferrara: 'As far as I'm concerned, *King of New York* is better than *Goodfellas*. That is about as pure a vision as you're going to imagine. I mean, that's exactly what Abel Ferrara wanted to do his entire career. It has the polish and the artistry of a pure vision and, at the same time, it's just *full on out* action.' It's also a favourite of Tim Roth's: 'I love violence in movies because it affects me, it hurts me... Ferrara's *King of New York* is part of that. Christopher Walken – the most unpredictable performance. You never knew if he was happy or sad. '

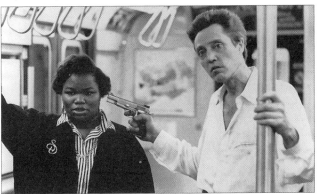

Christopher Walken – happy or sad? – in Abel Ferrara's King of New York *(1990).*

John Woo: As far as the 'action-adventure' sequences of Tarantino's movies go, John Woo is his oriental godfather. Belying the 'realist' tag that some mainstream film critics have tried to hang on Tarantino's violent scenes, Woo's example showed him how to adapt a basic in-your-face blood and bullets scene into something so cinematically stylised it became aesthetically beautiful.

Ride the Whirlwind *(above)* / The Shooting *(both 1966)*: Monte Hellman's elliptical, existential *westerns were shot back to back – a method that has appealed to Tarantino. His largely overlooked films inspired Tarantino, and Hellman was executive producer on* Reservoir Dogs.

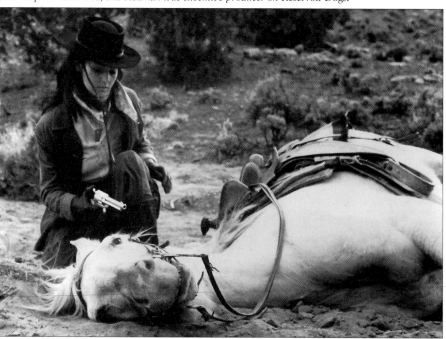

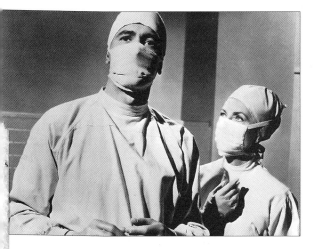

Magnificient Obsession *(1954), Tarantino's favourite romantic drama, is a typical, hysterically overwrought melodrama from director Douglas Sirk, with Rock Hudson as a playboy surgeon devoting his life to trying to restore the sight of a woman which he destroyed in a car accident, falling deeply in love with her in the process. Sirk is well-deserving of the 'Douglas Sirk steak' accolade in* Pulp Fiction – *the meat comes either bloody rare or fiercely overdone.*

Big Wednesday *(1978): 'I don't like surfers. I didn't like them when I was growing up. I grew up in a surfing community, I think they're all jerks. Alright… I like* Big Wednesday *so* much, *surfers don't deserve it.'*

Rolling Thunder *(1977) is written and directed by Paul Schrader, who also wrote* Taxi Driver *several years before it was produced, when he was experiencing a similar state of psychosis to its title character. Unsung inspiration to a host of lesser vigilante movies, like* The Exterminator, Rolling Thunder *also gave its title to Tarantino's new film distribution network, run via Miramax.*

*Lee Marvin in Don Siegel's
The Killers (1964). Vincent
and Jules' prototype in
Pulp Fiction: the classic
emotionless hitman in thin-
lapelled suit and skinny tie.*

*Poster artwork for
Where Eagles Dare (1970).
'Where Eagles Dare is my
personal favourite of the
guys-on-a-mission movie.
I love guy-on-a-mission
movies. I'm gonna make a
guys-on-a-mission movie
one day.'*

Above left: Winchester 73 (1950. One of the first of Anthony Mann's acclaimed 'psychological westerns' with James Stewart, bringing a subtle motivation to a lead character in the standard genre scenario. Tarantino's favourite traditional western.

Above right: One-Eyed Jacks (1961). 'If I had to pick the five greatest western directors of all time, the problem wouldn't be to pick five, but to figure out how many westerns a director had to make to be considered a western director. Does one film do it? Can I make a case for Marlon Brando, since One-Eyed Jacks is one of my five favourite westerns?'

Blaxploitation: 'Blaxploitation' translates as crime thrillers, mainly of 70s vintage, that featured afro-ed 'superspades' in the capacity of both hero and villain. Mostly produced and directed by whites (with honourable exceptions such as *Cotton Comes to Harlem*, adapted from the novel by armed-robber-turned-detective-fiction-writer Chester Himes), the pictures successfully catered for the black US audience, and other converts such as the young QT.

Tarantino's love of the genre was demonstrated by his appearance at 1994's Shots in the Dark crime film festival, in Nottingham, where a print of *Pulp Fiction* was premiered to little fanfare and much fan-worship. Adrian Wooton, the Shots in the Dark organiser, doubted the director would be able to make the festival due to a fraught promotional schedule, but the man turned up with his own selection of rare-as-hell blaxploitation

The Mack *(1973), directed by Michael Campus and starring Max Julien (above) and Richard Pryor, is Tarantino's favourite blaxploitation movie. 'A kind of pimp* Scarface*', it follows the rise and fall of a 'mack', or pimp. Apart from the standard flashy violence,* The Mack *imparts a sense of realism missing from most other blaxploitation epics.*

pictures, ever the obsessive grown-up fanboy. He introduced and spieled about such films as *The Spook Who Sat by the Door, Coffy* ('She's hot, black and she'll cream you!' prickteased the ads, showing Pam Grier not only as a mankiller, but a maneater), and *The Mack*, 'a kind of pimp *Scarface*,' informed, like some 1970s black gangster fiction and later gangster rap music, by the attitude of Iceberg Slim, author of *Pimp: The Story of My Life.*

Italian Exploitation Films: 'They used to be well distributed back in the 60s, but they showed up big time in the video explosion in the early 80s. It's stopping now, because there's no market for dubbed films in America… when they come out, they're really just thrown out there, y'know, they couldn't care less. But for a while there, video stores were buying everything, and that was when all this stuff got released… I actually worked for a company for a while – Imperial Entertainment – and they released a bunch of Italian stuff for a long time, so it was really cool. They released *Demons 2*, which was the biggest of all their Italian things; they also re-released some great Italian westerns, Duccio Tessari films like *The Return of Ringo*, and the first *Ringo* movie.'

Tarantino's Italian exploitation favourites: Argento, particularly *Suspiria* and *Two Evil Eyes*, which he feels are the only two of his movies that are good from beginning to end. 'I got into it, of course, through Mario Bava. After Bava I got into spaghetti westerns, guys like Sergio Sollima, who's fantastic, y'know: *Face To Face* and *The Big Gundown*… that one is a particular favourite of mine. Also Damiano Damiani, who did *A Bullet for the General* and *Confessions of a Police Captain* – with Franco Nero and

Opera *(above left)* /Suspiria *(top right)* *(1987): Tarantino's favourite* gialli *(Italian murder movies). Both directed by Dario Argento, whose convoluted, hackneyed, or downright silly plots are merely vehicles for his incredibly intense visuals – which really do make an art out of murder. As Tarantino says of his days as an aspiring actor/filmmaker, 'I would have learned Italian to work with Dario Argento.'*

*(**Above right**) Lee van Cleef with Anthony Dawson in the latter's* Take a Hard Ride *(1975).*

Martin Balsam – and *Amityville 2*. He's really good… Sergio Leone, naturally… Then I discovered Anthony Dawson (Antonio Margheriti)… the first movie where I knew I was watching an Anthony Dawson movie was *The Stranger and The Gunfighter*, the Lee Van Cleef/Lo Lieh kung fu western. I collect his films, I've got a pretty big Anthony Dawson collection now. A bunch of my friends and I are into a lot of his early movies, really neat stuff like *Castle of Blood* and *The Long Hair of Death*. But I think probably my favourite Anthony Dawson movie ever is *Cannibals in the Streets*. I also like *The Last Hunter*… it's hysterical, the way these movies have been released and re-released in America… y'know, Dawson did all these Vietnam movies, *The Last Hunter, Tornado*

Strike Force, all these things, and he did them before *Rambo*, they were all actually *Apocalypse Now* rip-offs. [The original Italian title of *Cannibals in the Streets* translates as *Apocalypse Tomorrow*.] *Rambo* is really well done and everything, but it has the flavour of an Anthony Dawson film... in America, they just re-released all his *Deer Hunter* rip-offs and marketed them as *Rambo* rip-offs!... Another Dawson movie I like is *Take a Hard Ride*, that's a cool one...'

'After all that stuff I started getting into the mafia movies, a whole stack of them, and the number one director was Fernando Di Leo – he's sort of like the Don Siegel of Italy, did a whole bunch of movies. There are two he did, *Rulers of the City* and another one called *Hitman*; *Rulers of the City* starred Jack Palance and *Hitman* starred Henry Silva and Woody Strode, and they've been retitled so many times in America, because they've released and re-released, so five different companies have them, all under different names... it's common to go into a video store and find that the owners have the same movie under different titles, and don't even know it's the same thing... *Rulers of the City* has been known as *Big Boss*, *Mr Scarface*, *The Sicilian Connection*... but Fernando Di Leo is really cool, *Hitman* is a really neat movie, and he did another one, one of my favourites from the Franco Nero action movies of the 70s, a film called *Street Law*, in which he stars with Barbara Bach. It's like a *Death Wish* kind of movie, and it's terrific, man! It is a great, great action film, it's just really wonderful – Franco Nero is the meek, mild guy, who's pushed into being a vigilante and stuff – really terrific! A lot of Di Leo's movies were really cool, because sometimes they'd get someone who was a big star in Italy like Franco Nero, Tomas Milian or someone like that, or sometimes they'd get an American star, like *Rico* with Christopher Mitchum, that's a good one... Robert Blake did a movie over there called *Ripped Off*, before *Barretta* had happened... whether or not they had an American actor or an Italian as the lead, they always had a fallen American actor playing the big mob guy – Martin Balsam or Lee J. Cobb or Richard Conte or Arthur Kennedy... Alain Delon did a good Italian movie that was released in America called *No Way Out*, that's really cool. Richard Conte is the mob guy in it, the *Big Boss Man*, he was really good... What's cool though is that when the mafia movies started, Sergio Sollima just switched from doing spaghetti westerns to doing mafia crime movies, and his best was *The Family* with Charles Bronson, Jill Ireland and Telly Savalas... I think it was known in Britain as *Violent City*, because the original title is *Citta Violenta*... it's terrific. What's wild about *The Family* is that it's a full-on remake, with the same story points and everything, of *Out of the Past*, the Jacques Tourneur/Robert Mitchum thing... Exact same story, but Bronson is a hitman as opposed to a detective... Sollima also did a remake of his own movie, *The Big Gundown*, in a modern setting, called *Revolver*. It's got many titles on video, I've got it as *Blood on the Streets*. Oliver Reed's in the Lee Van Cleef role, and Fabio Tosa in the Tomas Milian role... There's one of the Italian mafia movies, I'm trying to remember if Fernando Di Leo did it or not, but it's a great one with Helmut Berger, called *Mad Dog*. It's terrific, and it's got Helmut Berger as the bad guy, and he totally lives up to the title, just an out of control crazy hitman killer, and this cop's after him... it's a really cool movie, it's so neat.'

'Other guys I like are Alberto De Martino, Duccio Tessari... De Martino is just great. [Director of *Strange Shadows in an Empty Room*, starring John Saxon, Martin Landau and Tisa Farrow, and featuring a kung fu fight with a gang of transvestites in a penthouse on top of a skyscraper.] I love De Martino: *Holocaust 2000*'s good, *The Tempter...*'

'[*Stage Fright* is] better than anything Argento's ever done. The only thing that can touch it is some of the sequences in *Terror at the Opera*. I love *Opera*. It doesn't work from beginning to end like *Stage Fright* does, but some of the sequences – you know, the first time they do the "needles under the eyes" thing, wow! But for my money, in the 80s, *Stage Fright* is the best Italian horror film, and Michele (Soavi) is the most talented guy on the Italian film scene right now...'

Tarantino claims not to know where the overt influences of the Hong Kong thrillers and Italian mafia movies rear their heads in his work.

'What's happened recently is that the people who work in the crime genre now, the directors, are kind of becoming the stars of the movies. Horror film directors were like that in the 1970s. If you were a horror film geek, you went and saw George Romero's movies, John Carpenter's movies, Dario Argento's movies. They were the stars, the heroes. That's not necessarily the case right now for horror films – they don't make that many any more. But in some ways John Woo and Abel Ferrara and 'Beat' Takeshi – they've taken that slot. So it's kind of an exciting time to do those movies.'

'The thing about crime films, in particular, is that the yakuza movies they make in Japan, the triad movies they make in Hong Kong, the Italian mafia movies, Jean-Pierre Melville's films in France... the thing is, we're all telling the same stories, but we're all telling them differently, because we're all from different cultures, different nationalities, and that's what's really interesting to me, how different cultures attack the same story. The story's almost exactly the same in every country, y'know: the hitman's supposed to do something for someone, but he doesn't do it, so they kill his girlfriend, and he goes to get the Big Boss... in Japan they do it differently, in Hong Kong they do it differently. I'm familiar with all this stuff because I've been watching it my whole life... got the job in the video store because I'm like a film expert... Hey, they don't teach you "The films of Anthony Dawson" at UCLA!'

'The thing about guys like Dawson or what's his name, Enzo G. Castellari, or whatever, is that those guys do like a zillion movies, and I get a kick out of those films because in the case of those guys, and in particular Dawson – I mean the guy's a hack but he's a hack who really knows what he's doing – you're in good hands and they're real fun, and Castellari... he did a load of disposable stuff like *The Bronx Warriors* and all those *Mad Max*-type movies, but I think he's probably also the director who's worked with Franco Nero more than anybody... The crime/action movies they did together are really good. He did one movie – and I think it's one of the best movies in all Italian expoitation – *The Inglorious Bastards!*... they're American soldiers who have been condemned to death and they escape, so they're trying to get to neutral Switzerland, trying to carve their way out, fighting both the Americans and the Nazis... It's terrific, it really is, really good, and the script is fantastic. It's like a homage to Sam Peckinpah's *Cross of Iron*, which was a smash in Italy, so they made a bunch of *Cross of Iron* rip-offs and that's what this movie, stylistically, is taking its cue off.'

'I always follow all those trends, in fact the only one I don't follow that much – because they really didn't do them that well though they did them forever – is those post-apocalypse *Mad Max* rip-offs. I love *Mad Max*, though... But one of those post-apocalyptic movies I did like was about these guys attempting to repopulate the earth, Martin Dolman's (Sergio Martino's) *After the Fall of New York*... Martino did a great job... George Eastman's in it as "The Big Ape", and there was this one guy in the movie, I don't recall his name, but he's the guy who's protecting the girl once he's found her, and it's great because he's kind of like an Italian William Smith... I see him crop up all the time, he's kind of a real big guy with sandy-coloured hair and he just looks like an Italian William Smith. He leads some rebel crowd in it, and when he finds this woman, the last fertile woman, he protects her, that kind of thing... I also get a big kick out of the *Thunder Warrior* series.'

With Tarantino's tastes falling decidedly on the carnivorous side, his liking for cannibal movies almost equals his love of cheeseburgers. Despite great affection for *Cannibals in the Streets*, he confirms, '*Cannibal Holocaust* is my favourite, a really cool film.'

'I like a lot of the zombie movies, like *City of the Walking Dead* (*Nightmare City*),

The Inglorious Bastards *(1978), a story of renegade US soldiers trying to fight off both the Wehrmacht and their own side, directed by Enzo G. Castellari. Tarantino rates it as among the best Italian exploitation movies.*

The Gates of Hell *(known as* City of the Living Dead *in the UK; 1981): One of the main factors endearing Tarantino to Italian exploitation movies is their 'sense of over-the-topness'. There are few more over-the-top movie-makers than spaghetti horror master Lucio Fulci, who made this as the first of his 'Gates of Hell' trilogy. As the bowels of Hell rise up in a New England town, Signor Fulci lets go of all restraint. People cry tears of blood; one young woman pukes up her vital organs. As with other Fulci horror movies – such as* Zombie *– Gates of Hell was, unsurprisingly, banned in the UK in its uncut form, as a 'video nasty'.*

the Umberto Lenzi one... I just love the fact that the zombies in this movie run, shoot machine guns... it's like – fuck man, it's no fun being chased by a zombie and he can run as fast as you! That's so cool, and it was such a neat idea, based on the whole *Nosferatu* thing, to have the plane landing with all these zombies in it... really cool, and I had a lot of fun with it. I get a big kick out of all those zombie movies. The only problem I have with *Zombie (Flesh Eaters)* is the fact that people in it don't turn round fast enough! Me and my friends were watching the movie, and we all agreed that if you were in this jungle full of flesh eating zombies, OK, and they turn up behind you, guys in the movies always turn around like v-e-r-y slowly; I would be like the Jesse Owens man, the Carl fucking Lewis of turning around... *Zombie* has one of the most out-of-control scenes I've ever seen in my life! It's the scene where the zombie falls to the bottom of the ocean floor, and he's just tripping along, minding his own business, and a shark comes to eat him! So he starts eating the shark! Now what's weird about that scene is that while you're watching it, it actually makes a little sense, but when you try and describe this scene to someone who hasn't seen the movie, they just go: "What? That was in a movie?!?" and you say: "Yeah, I suppose it sounds pretty wild," but in the movie it seems like a real commonplace. But my favourite Fulci is *Gates of Hell (City of the*

Living Dead)... House by the Cemetery is also great fun, it has that great sequence where the kid's head is held against the door while his father is on the other side trying to smash through it with an axe. That's more or less a replay of the scene in *Gates of Hell* where they're digging up the girl, which I actually think, along with the zombie/shark fight, is the best sequence Fulci's ever done. I really love John Morghen [star of *Cannibals in the Streets* and *Cannibal Ferox*] in that film too, he's such a cool character.' (He's a prepossessing but unlikely ladies' man, living in a shack with a blow-up doll and a decomposing baby.)

'They [Italian exploitation movies] are an acquired taste, and you have to forgive a lot of things in them, but they're fun and I just like the kind of operatic feel that they bring to it... I get such a kick out of them, because they go crazy with all these zooms and everything... the sense of over-the-topness in them is really cool, really neat, and I like the fact that you're into a brand of cinema that not everyone in the world is into... it's like being in this select little club!'

The man who would be King Geek

First proof that Tarantino had finally arrived came in January 1994. His longtime agent, Cathryn James, was clearing up the debris of her office on the morning following the LA earthquake. A call came on the still-functional phone from Tarantino's new business adviser, hired for him by Ms James. The message was almost designed to add to those Richter Scale blues: the word from her protegé was that her services were no longer required, from that day forth.

According to Cathryn James, when she finally got to speak to Tarantino himself on the matter, he was almost incredulous that she believed she had a grievance: 'You can't be upset. You're the best manager in the world. Your job was to launch my career – well, my career is launched and your job is done. I don't need you anymore. Anyway, what made you think I would stay with you?' 'Well,' she replied, 'because you said you would.'

Her client of nine years standing didn't appreciate those tactics. 'You can't hold me to that. Who d'you think you are, the Devil calling in a contract?'

Any parties who knew both James and Tarantino looked on in surprise, if not dismay. 'She paid his rent, she supported him and she put up with all the rejection letters,' said Don Murphy, producer of *Natural Born Killers*. (Tarantino denies that Cathryn James ever paid his rent – though he has no problems with acknowledging she'd throw him five bucks, or take him out to dinner, whenever he needed support.) 'And the moment he gets some success, he fires her.'

'Quentin has forgotten the people who helped him when he hadn't made it,' said Stanley Margolis, the business manager who was the first person to buy a Tarantino script.

'I was emotionally stricken. I'd invested ten years of my life in Quentin. But I've gotten past it now. My business is fine. There is life after Quentin,' says Cathryn James herself. 'I hate to use the word "disappointed", but in his case it applies. I have a very deep feeling for him. He's like a wayward nephew. But I'm so ashamed of him for not being a more gracious human being. Lots of people supported him and helped him. He could afford to acknowledge them.'

Someone Cathryn James believes came in for shoddy treatment is one Craig Hamann, a writer now entering his mid-40s. Hamann was one of Tarantino's inner circle of fellow movie geeks and enthusiast friends for ten years, the two of them first meeting at James Best's acting school: 'We were all movie junkies. For me one of the most delightful things in life was to go to the movies with Quentin.' He was much involved with his younger friend's career aspirations in the early days, to the extent of co-financing (alongside Connie, Tarantino's mother) and co-writing *My Best Friend's Birthday*, the abortive first attempt at a feature.

Hamann also makes much of the fact that he corrected and typed scripts for Tarantino in the early days – 'Quentin can't spell. He doesn't make any bones about that. I typed up scripts and stuff. We went over things together, read dialogue together. I

Zombie (Flesh Eaters; 1980): *When Lucio Fulci's delicate film was shown on the West Coast, audiences were furnished with sick bags. Apart from the scene which blew Tarantino's mind, where a zombie fights a shark underwater, the movie is distinguished by probably the most flinch-inducing shot ever filmed, showing a spike entering an eye.*

thought he was brilliant right from the start. The first script he brought to me was entitled *Open Road*, which was *True Romance* and *Natural Born Killers* combined. I helped him out with screenplay structure. We helped each other a lot.'

Factually, this may be irrefutable, but the moment an editor is considered ultimately responsible for a writer's work is the day that boxing promoter Don King, not Mike Tyson, is the true uncrowned world heavyweight champion.

As Tarantino says, 'There's nothing wrong with feeling jealous of someone's situation, that's just human. But when you have someone who thinks that your success is their failure, that's really fucked up.'

That said, there's little doubt that Tarantino has no inhibitions about calling up friends when he reaches a sticking point. Hamann jokes that he was 'drug consultant' for *Pulp Fiction*, called upon to work on script details, give directorial advice and help coach the actors for the scene hingeing on Uma Thurman's heroin overdose. His contribution went uncredited. Similarly unequivocal is the fact that Hamann doctored a very basic early Tarantino script outline (or treatment) entitled *Criminal Mind*, to the point where he became a collaborator: 'He'd got a treatment, handwritten as usual, and he had the first two acts. I took it home, typed it up, structured it, added a third act and brought it back to him.'

The premise – that a serial killer defies the established behavioural patterns and suddenly stops killing, leaving the primary cop on his case ever more obsessed with catching him – sounds promising, but seems to call for the dogged Thomas Harris approach to law-enforcement procedure that made *The Silence of the Lambs* ring with authenticity. Little wonder, perhaps, that Tarantino has long since abandoned the idea. Maybe less understandable is why he absolutely forbids Hamann to take over the concept of *Criminal Mind*, and expand the treatment into a script.

'This is a cold-hearted, unforgiving business,' says Hamann. 'If you don't figure that out, you won't make it. Quentin has figured it out. On a personal level, though, there's a code that he's just danced around. Quentin will take a piece of something I've written, or a large piece of something Roger's written. It might be nice if he asked first.'

Tarantino's first extra-curricular acting role was in Rory Kelly's *Sleep With Me* (1994), playing a movie geek named Sid who expounds a theory on the homo-erotic sub-text of *Top Gun*. Supposedly, his own theory...

After shooting *Killing Zoe* (see below), Roger Avary was having dinner with the movie's lead, Eric Stoltz, then starring in *Sleep With Me*, for which he also acted as producer. Avary was going into a standard anecdote of his which amused all his friends, about how the fighter-pilot character played by Tom Cruise in Tony Scott's *Top Gun* is a repressed gay, and the movie is all about his coming to terms with homosexuality. Somehow, the spiel didn't get the desired response. Stoltz's expression went aghast, and he covered his mouth in horror. When asked what the matter was, he replied that he'd just heard Quentin 'improvise' that exact speech while giving his cameo performance in *Sleep With Me*.

Despite the movie's lack of success, the speech itself achieved cult status, like most everything Tarantino has touched. At the London National Film Theatre appearance, he talked to the audience about the autobiographical thread running through his characters, and how the opinions they express often reflect his own. For instance, he told the audience, to appreciative laughter, 'I do believe that is the subtext of *Top Gun*.'

Well he might, but the authorship of the opinion clearly rankles with Roger Avary. 'Whoever writes a scene first, gets it,' Tarantino once told him – sound advice for any budding writer. Anyone who ignores material that's ripe for the picking, in day-to-day life, the news media, books, movies, or wherever, deprives himself of stimuli. Even the reinterpretation of other's ideas remains valid, as long as (as we've seen with Tarantino) it carries an element of originality, of personal statement. How close *Sleep With Me's Top Gun* spiel is to Avary's anecdotal source is a moot point – though there's little doubt Tarantino played up the actual expression of the idea to his usual showmanish degree. Avary shows no inclination to enter any battle with his longtime friend, and sometime collaborator, over use of his ideas, though he says, 'I've realised I can't hang out with Quentin. If I talk with him, he sucks stuff from me. I'm glad he's successful and I hope he doesn't fall on his face. But if he does, every single person he's hurt will be there for him.'

Avary's Zoe

In the wake of *Reservoir Dogs*, Tarantino did at least help his old friend take the helm on a feature film of his own.

'Lawrence [Bender] called me up when they were scouting locations for *Dogs*,' Avary recalls, 'and said, "Oh my God, we've found this great bank, and you've gotta come down and check it out. We have no use for it in *Dogs*, but it's a great location." So I went down, and he said, "If you have any scripts that take place in a bank, we could kick together a hundred or two hundred thousand dollars and make a movie here."'

According to Bender, Avary responded with an ingenious pragmatism that at an earlier point in American cinema would have earned him a prolific career at the head of a B-movie production line: 'Roger didn't even skip a beat. He goes, "Oh yeah, I was just thinking about an idea that takes place in a bank."'

'So I drew a map of the bank and went home,' says Avary, 'and wrote the script in about a week, week and a half... It's like what Roger Corman used to do: "Oh, we've

Below left: Killing Zoe (1994). In Roger Avary's heist movie the doomed Eric (Jean-Hugues Anglade) and Zed (Eric Stoltz) make unrealistic demands from within the bank that Eric's gang have overrun.

Above: Killing Zoe: Zoe (Julie Delpy) comforts Zed, who has come to rob the bank in which she works, after he has been attacked by Eric.

got a prison set and we've got the Tropicana girls – we should do a women-in-prison film!" He'd find a young Jonathan Demme, or Jonathan Kaplan, or Joe Dante, or Francis Coppola, or Martin Scorsese, and just because they were so hungry to make a movie, they'd make the best women-in-prison film ever. A lot of Corman films are exploitation films, but they're also arthouse films.'

Avary gave himself much to live up to, by invoking Corman's old creative roster. However, once Bender started hawking the project around it seemed to have legs – though whether the selling point was the script itself, or his close connections with Tarantino and his producer, is hard to discern. Chief producer of Avary's project would be Samuel Hadida, the Paris-based exploitation producer, instrumental in bringing the budget up to a level that would at least pay wages for a professional cast and crew. Much as it's likely he saw European potential in a hardboiled crime thriller set in Paris

Le Doulos *(1962), French gangster movie in* film noir *style by Jean-Pierre Melville. Avary beat Tarantino in paying homage to the gallic thrillers they both admired. Tarantino says the enigmatic nature of* Le Doulos – *where the story behind the action is concealed till the last 20 minutes – was a big influence on the unfolding narrative of* Reservoir Dogs.

(interiors for the movie would be shot in the USA, exteriors taken in the French capital), his awareness of Avary's part in writing *True Romance*, and the immense bankability of his partner's name, can only have helped the second Video Archives graduate's case.

In fact about all the movie has in common with Tarantino's works, except for its central heist, is the genre-bound nature of Avary's script, where every character exists as an archetype or stereotype, or simply in order to move the story along. The genre which Avary pays tribute to is the French crime thriller of the late 50s to early 80s. This, in turn, took its inspiration from pulp-influenced US thrillers of the 40s and 50s, which critics in the film journal *Cahiers du Cinema* christened '*film noir*', in tribute to their shadowy neo-expressionist cinematography, as well as to the black plotlines involving desperate men and women with no way out.

Jean-Pierre Melville was the first French director to make a career of appropriating American thriller imagery – re-inventing Paris as a dangerous city where life was cheap and love was bitter – and in placing his crime movie back in lowlife Paris, Avary beat Tarantino to the post in honouring Melville – and any other French moviemakers who dealt in hardboiled cinema – in the way he paid homage to his own *noir* sources.

Tarantino's only involvement with *Killing Zoe*, despite the comparisons made by critics with his own work, was purely on a business basis, using his name to help Avary raise the money, as was also the case with Lawrence Bender. Tarantino claims to have lent his name to the project without a fee, and says that he knows the director would have dispensed with any *Reservoir Dogs*-related publicity, had it been in his power.

Before shooting *Killing Zoe*, Avary had flown to Amsterdam to work with Tarantino on the first draft of *Pulp Fiction*. Avary's main contribution is the second story, appearing at the centre of screen time. The younger writer/director observes, however, that there was no mention of heroin – le drug nihil, that plays such a huge role in Parisian lowlife – before his one-time partner/now mentor saw a rough cut of *Killing Zoe*. Some animated bubbles viewed by the opiated Zed in *Killing Zoe* are also echoed, more innocently, by a cartoon square Uma Thurman draws in the air in *Pulp Fiction*. This cute little effect wasn't in the original *Pulp* script, once again apparently not added till Tarantino saw the rough cut of *Zoe*.

Soon after, the seductively lethal opiate became a major story device in the most controversial and highly lauded part of the movie.

Mia (Uma Thurman), showing that alcohol is not her drug of choice, enjoys a milk shake in a night club with Vincent, in Pulp Fiction.

Tarantino on the set of Pulp Fiction.

CHAPTER 5

Pulp Fiction – 'Let's get into character'

' In the case of *Pulp Fiction*,' remembers its central (but not sole) creator, 'the starting-off point, the jumping-off point for the piece, was the idea of doing a crime film anthology – you know, I've never seen a crime film anthology. And yet these were like the most done in paperbacks, like in *Black Mask* magazine and stuff. And so I thought of doing it in a film, but on sitting down I realised, "Well yeah, that's fun to do, but there's much more gold here." It would be really neat to have three separate stories, but have the same three characters floating in and out.'

Roger Avary remembers the genesis of *Pulp Fiction* as the aftermath of another frustrating meeting with Stanley Margolis, discussing the logjammed *True Romance*. After he and Tarantino had left the office, walking down a nearby boulevard, they hit on the idea of diverting their creative energies towards an anthology of three connected short films. One section each would be written by half of the Tarantino/Avary partnership, with one more by an unspecified third writer. All three would be joined by the idea of a subversive take on old pulp-thriller ideas, the project provisionally entitled *The Black Mask*, in tribute to the seminal pulp crime magazine.

Tarantino remarked to Avary on the basic competitiveness of the format (eventually to be followed more fully to the letter by *Four Rooms*, despite the difference in theme), how one writer's segment was bound to overshadow the others'. For his contribution Tarantino first planned a claustrophobic ensemble piece based around a failed robbery, which expanded in scope to become his first feature.

Initially, rights for Tarantino's ambitious second feature rested with Tristar Pictures. The deal was struck as early as 1991, on the back of positive reports emanating from the *Reservoir Dogs* set. By late '93, with the script completed – all written at Tarantino's apartment in Amsterdam, apart from the original Avary contributions that were revised there – and *Dogs* a major European success, Harvey Weinstein of Miramax, *Dogs*' distributors, stepped in to buy out the project from a nervous Tristar. Having recently been acquired by the Walt Disney Corporation, Miramax would offer Tarantino's compendium of hardboiled American lowlife tales as their first feature for the family entertainment multi-national. Despite having bailed out of *True Romance* when the budget passed $20 million, Weinstein was now proud to announce that Miramax was 'in the Quentin Tarantino business'. Still modestly budgeted, by Hollywood standards, at

$8 million, the deal was co-financed by a new production company, Danny De Vito's Jersey Films.

'I always wanna make sure I put the money on the screen,' Tarantino claims. 'On *Reservoir Dogs*, we shot the movie for $1.5 million but I wanted it to look like an $8 million movie. With *Pulp* we had $8 million, but I wanted it to look like an epic. I wanted it to look like a $20-$25 million movie. It's an epic in everything, in invention, in tension, in ambition, in length, in scope, in everything except the price tag.'

By the time of *Pulp Fiction*'s production, no-one but no-one was in a position to outshine Quentin Tarantino. Avary's original story – *Pandemonium Reigns*, a variation on the old chestnut about the boxer who refuses to throw the fight – remains crucially woven into the narrative fabric, but the movie itself was produced on the basis that it was the second picture to be both written and directed by the creator of *Reservoir Dogs*. Tarantino exercised an auteur-like control over the movie. But Avary's co-writer status cannot be denied. In fact, two of Avary's excised scenes from the original *True Romance* screenplay were assimilated by Tarantino into the new context – the accidental firing-off of a gun inside a car, splattering the backseat passenger's brains all over the upholstery, and the emergence of a hidden gunman from the bathroom where he's been hiding, firing off a volley of shots at his target but missing with each one.

Tarantino's explanation of how he assimilated Avary's work into the movie is straightforward enough: 'When I finished *Dogs*, I decided to do *Pulp Fiction*, so I bought Roger's script. I was going to write it first and then bring Roger in to do the final draft together. But in the meantime, I got the idea to overlap the characters, so I adapted Roger's screenplay, like you'd adapt a novel.'

In the final days of Tarantino's international film festival tour, he returned to LA and was staying at the Avarys' home. Avary was by then editing *Killing Zoe*, and dangerously close to running out of money. 'All of a sudden,' says Avary, 'Quentin decided he wanted the full credit on *Pulp Fiction* – he's really into full authorship. I said, "No, I won't give up the script credit." But I needed money. I was owed another $27,000, but he didn't have to [pay] until he started shooting, and he wasn't due to begin for six months. He said, "I'll give you that money now, if you sign this paper." And I did.'

The paper was a 'back-end' deal agreement, guaranteeing a substantial share in the film's profits. Even so, it had dawned on Avary that his name was never going to become synonymous with any of the work he'd done with his former partner.

'I always thought it didn't matter whose idea it was – what mattered was the movie. Now I realise that's not the case. People do care.' None more so than Tarantino himself. It was obvious to him that a career doesn't thrive on work alone, but on kudos. He knew *Pulp Fiction* had to appear first and foremost in the public consciousness as A Quentin Tarantino Film.

The pre-credits sequence is preceded by two dictionary definitions of 'pulp": cheap paper and cheap literature.

Pre-credits: two English lovers sit in an LA coffee shop/diner. Referring to each other as 'Pumpkin' and 'Honey Bunny', they discuss how their life of crime together is going to have to change – liquor stores are too much risk, not enough profit, while banks are slightly beyond their capacity. Hitting on an idea, they jump to their feet and hold up the diner.

POST-CREDITS PROLOGUE

Two identically dressed men – Jules, who's black, and Vincent, white – are exchanging smalltalk about Vincent's recent stay in Europe. Carrying on their conversation as they stop and unload two .45 automatic pistols from the back of their car, it's clear they've come to perform an assassination. Vincent complains that they should have been issued shotguns for the job, unsure of how many men they're going to have hit, but persists in his enquiries about Tony Rocky Horror, a Samoan friend of theirs, who was thrown from his apartment balcony for the apparent crime of giving their boss's wife a foot massage. Jules enquires why he's so hung up on the story, to be told by Vincent that he has been asked by Marsellus, their boss, to look after Mia, his wife, while her husband is out of town. Vincent is nervous about keeping everything above board.

Inside the apartment they invade, they find three young men about to dig into their breakfast from the local Hawaiian burger bar. The most vocal member, Brett, who's as terrified as all the others, gives back a case containing some mysterious glowing commodity that they've stolen from Marsellus. He tries to talk his way out of it, but is put in his place by Jules, who is running the show, even to the point of stealing their breakfast. Jules delivers his standard assassination speech – a retributive sermon from the Book of Ezekiel – then he and Vincent open fire.

VINCENT VEGA AND MARSELLUS WALLACE'S WIFE

Afternoon. In a near-empty club owned by himself, Marsellus Wallace is giving a pep talk to Butch, a boxer, on taking a dive in the fifth round of his forthcoming title fight. Butch agrees, and Marsellus is alerted to the arrival of Vincent and Jules by the barman. Both are dressed in gaudy t-shirts and shorts, and Jules doesn't want to talk about what happened to their normally dapper clothes. Vincent behaves obnoxiously towards the boxer up at the bar, only a call from Marsellus dissuading the fighter from punching him out.

In a domestic apartment, Vincent sits listening to a young woman tell her girlfriend about the metal piercings she has through parts of her body. A true Californian 'modern primitive', her rings exceed the standard ear/nose/eyebrow combination, extending to her nipples and even her clitoris. The man of the house, Lance, comes to do business with Vincent. Vincent has come to score heroin, and settles for the most expensive brand on offer, which Lance promises is a 'fuckin' madman'. During a polite conversation Vincent complains about the paintwork of his car being maliciously scratched after being out of storage for only five days; Lance apparently shares his outrage. Vincent asks if he can shoot up in Lance's bathroom, and is granted permission.

At the Wallaces' home, Vincent arrives to take Mia, his boss's wife, out for the evening. The place is controlled by a high-tech security network of cameras and intercoms. As

Vincent waits, listening to her powerful stereo as he takes a drink, Mia watches him on a closed-circuit. She snorts cocaine – a ritual which will be repeated all night long – and they're ready to go.

Jack Rabbit Slim's, a 1950s diner-style 'theme restaurant": Vincent and Mia's conversation is stilted at first, Vincent feeling ill at ease with the surroundings, but gradually loosens up. Mia appears to be showing a restrained interest in her escort. She goes to the ladies' room to snort more cocaine, and, on return, insists they enter the restaurant's dancing competition, hosted by an Ed Sullivan lookalike on a big stage. Vincent refuses, but Mia pulls rank as the boss's wife. They dance to a Chuck Berry number; she as animated as he's opiated, both losing their inhibitions.

They return home to the Wallace residence. Both are elated about having won the dance contest, and have clearly had a great time. Vincent goes to take a leak, all the time lecturing himself on how he's going to be on his best behaviour and quietly excuse himself from Mia's company soon. Mia goes searching through Vincent's pocket, to find the tobacco pouch he used to roll her a cigarette back at the restaurant. She finds a plastic bag full of white powdered heroin and gets excited, believing it to be cocaine. Cutting it and snorting a line of it, she immediately overdoses and goes into an open-eyed coma. On return, Vincent is bewildered by what's happened but terrified when he realises the truth. Hauling the dying Mia into his car, he phones Lance, interrupting his stoned suburban domesticity. Lance refuses to help, telling Vincent to get her to hospital then call a lawyer, only to have Vincent's car skid to a halt on his front lawn. The hitman warns him that if he lets Marsellus Wallace's wife die, they'll be facing the wrath of the big man together. Reluctantly Lance lets them both in, calling on his wife, Jody – the body piercing fetishist – to fetch an emergency adrenalin shot he keeps in the refrigerator. Never having had to perform the revival shot before, he looks for his medical book but has to improvise instead. Insisting Vincent performs the flesh-crawling task, he draws a spot to mark the position of her heart, and instructs him to stab the hypo as hard as he can through her breastplate, then push down hard on the plunger. Mia revives, instantly and manically, like an electrified epileptic.

Arriving back home, a groggy Mia and a drained Vincent agree that Marsellus can go quite happily through the rest of his life without hearing about this little incident.

THE GOLD WATCH

A little boy named Butch is visited in the family home by a soldier named Captain Koons. Distracting the boy's attention from the TV, the soldier gives an emotional speech about the family heirloom he's brought home from Vietnam for him – a gold watch. The watch was passed down by the boy's great-grandfather, a WW1 veteran, and was secreted up the ass of his father, a POW of the Vietcong who died in captivity. Koons then hid it up his own rear end.

The adult Butch snaps awake from the dream of his childhood. He's now the boxer we saw being paid to throw the fight, which is about to begin.

The aftermath of the fight (which remains unseen): there's consternation among Marsellus and his men, as Butch has ratted on the deal and quite literally gone for the kill. (Mia, who's accompanying her husband, takes the opportunity to quietly thank Vincent for dinner.)

Christopher Walken, in his cameo role in Pulp
Fiction *(1994) as his father's friend returning
from Vietnam to tell the young Butch about the
gold watch he is about to entrust to him...*

*... and Butch awakening from the childhood
memory, realising that family honour prevents
him throwing the fight.*

Butch escapes from the changing room via a back window, and is picked up by a
Colombian lady cab driver. The sports report plays on the radio, and she asks him, quite
innocently, whether he's the boxer who beat his opponent to death that night. He reveals that
he is and a $100 fare buys her loyalty.

Back at his motel room, Butch tells his French girlfriend, Fabienne, the result of the
fight. (She hates the sport, and won't listen to any fight commentary.) He also tells her that
his opponent has retired from the game like him, which assures that it's all going to have a
happy ending. They're both aware, however, that they have to take their money and get out
of town in one piece for the happy ending to become reality. It's also apparent that Fabby is
the only person in Butch's life who is treated with any tenderness, and their touchingly
childish banter ends with them making love.

In the morning, as they're getting ready to leave, Butch finds out that Fabby packed
everything else, but left his gold watch back at their apartment. Flying into a violent rage, he
starts wrecking the room, but calms down by reminding himself that he never stressed to her
the heirloom's importance. He resolves to return and retrieve it, telling her to go and have
breakfast and that he'll be back soon.

Butch drives to the apartment in Fabby's little Honda. Back home, he finds his watch.
Everything's quiet; he's reassured enough to go and grab some breakfast, but he's startled to
find a submachine gun resting on his kitchen unit. The toilet flushes, and Butch goes to
confront the intruder. Vincent Vega, exiting the toilet, freezes. Butch holds the gun on him,
stock-still, until the noise of the toaster jerks him into action. Vincent is blown all over the
bathroom.

Out on the street, Marsellus, exiting from Teriyaki Donut with a bag of doughnuts and
coffee (Vincent was apparently no longer working with Jules), double-takes as he crosses the
path of Butch's car. Panicked, Butch drives at him and knocks him down, crashing as he
speeds away from the scene. Marsellus revives from temporary unconsciousness, surrounded
by a crowd of do-gooding onlookers. He takes out his pistol and fires at Butch, who's

clambering groggily from the car, but hits a woman onlooker instead. Butch doubles down a backstreet, taking refuge in the Mason Dixon Pawnshop. Marsellus enters, to be smacked in the face by a combination of punches from Butch who knocks him down and takes out his gun. About to blow him away, he's held at riflepoint by the redneck manager of the store. Knocking Butch out with the gunbutt, he goes to phone his partner, claiming 'Nobody kills anybody in my place of business except me or Zed.' When Zed arrives, the two prisoners are tied and bound, and it's suddenly apparent that they've stepped through a portal into some kind of sado-masochistic underground. The big man is chosen to be their first plaything, and 'the Gimp' – an emaciated little humanoid dressed from head to toe in black leather bondage wear – is released from a box where they keep him prisoner, to stand guard over Butch while still kept on a leash himself. While the two hillbillies are having fun tying down and sodomising the struggling Marsellus, Butch works his way free from his bonds and punches the gimp out, who is then hanged by his leash. Butch finds the store keys and goes to leave, but something makes him turn back. Taking a samurai sword from the various pieces of pawnshop junk, he enters the room where Marsellus is being raped and instantly disembowels Maynard, the first redneck. Zed, who is still astride Marsellus, clambers off to reach his victim's .45, challenged by Butch to grab for it and die. Marsellus intervenes with Maynard's shotgun, shooting Zed in the crotch. Butch asks what their situation is, Marsellus tells him there's no situation as long as he stays out of town and never tells anyone what happened to him. Zed, who's writhing in agony on the floor, is promised even more pain before he dies, courtesy of 'a couple of pipe-hitting niggers who'll go to work on the homes here with a pair of pliers and a blowtorch'.

Butch rides away on Zed's chopper, to take Fabby to a new life.

THE BONNIE SITUATION

Recap of the assassination of Brett, from the Prologue. The story moves on. After he and one of his compadres are blown away, a fourth man emerges from the bathroom where he's been hiding, firing off a full round of shots point blank from a Magnum. To everyone's total amazement, not a single shot hits either Jules or Vincent, the bullets embedding themselves in the wall. The two hitmen pause for a moment in stunned silence before blowing the fourth man away. While Vincent chides Marvin, a black kid who's the only survivor, for not squealing about the hidden gunmen, Jules starts talking about divine intervention. Vincent tries to make him lay off the mystical jive, but the conversation continues down at the car, where Marvin is taken along for the ride as a hostage before the police show up.

In the car Jules and Vincent argue about the spiritual meaning of what they've just experienced. Vincent can't believe he's hearing Jules tell him that he's quitting the Life, sardonically leaning over the backseat to ask Marvin for his opinion. As he does so, his finger accidentally tightens on the trigger of the gun he's fingering, which fires off a volley of shots and blows Marvin all over the car. With a crisis on their hands, Jules calls up a buddy named Jimmie, the only friend he can think of this side of town, asking to be able to take refuge temporarily at his place. Jimmie accedes, but is less than thrilled when they park a car with a bloody interior and a corpse in his garage. Their timetable is dictated by the return

Vincent (John Travolta) turns up at Jimmie's, messy from the results of his loose finger.

from work of his wife Bonnie, a night-nurse, in an hour and a half. Jules phones Marsellus for help, explaining that there's no way she can come home from work and find 'a bunch of gangsters doin' gangster shit in her kitchen'. Marsellus tells him he's putting 'the Wolf' onto it, and Jules is visibly relieved.

Winston Wolf – the Wolf – is a dapper criminal and a social animal. He tears himself away from a cocktail party, jotting down the basic elements of 'the Bonnie situation' in order to know how to deal with it. When he arrives at Jimmie's he rubs Vincent up the wrong way with his curtness, but the gunman is put back in his place by a reminder that they do everything within a set time or they end up doing time. With the expertise of an industrial cleaner, he has them remove all immediately visible signs of the body from the car, dispose of their own blood-spattered clothes and change into some of Jimmie's casual wear. (Jules wears an 'I'm with stupid' t-shirt.) Delivering their Chevrolet to Monster Joe's Truck and Tow, with whose earthy daughter he's apparently having an affair, he leaves Jules and Vincent to take a cab back home. They decide to go for breakfast instead.

EPILOGUE
In a coffee house diner Vincent and Jules debate the pros and cons of eating pork, before getting back onto the subject of whether Jules is seriously going to quit the Life. Jules insists that, miracle or not, he's had a spiritual revelation and there's no way for him to turn back. Then, they suddenly find themselves in the middle of the coffee-house raid that began in the pre-credits sequence. Pumpkin and Honey Bunny work their way around the tables, collecting wallets and valuables from the customers, intimidating the manager. They get to Jules, who refuses to show them what's in the briefcase he and Vincent retrieved from the Brett pack. Pumpkin insists, but all the audience – or any other character – sees is the mysterious glowing light and the robber's amazed expression. Jules takes advantage and rams his .45 under Pumpkin's chin, holding him hostage while Honey Bunny – who has the quaint old English name of Yolanda – makes hysterical threats. Jules calms her down, explaining how he and Vincent – who wants to shoot "em both – could handle this situation without too much trouble, but as he's starting a new life, he'd prefer for it not to end in bloodshed. He gives his sermon from Ezekiel, but as a rationalisation for mercy rather than retribution this time. As a reward for leaving the mysterious briefcase alone, he gives them his wallet, containing $1500, tells them to take all the money they've stolen and go. After a moment's hesitation, they run for it. Vincent, nonplussed, complains that his coffee is now cold, so both men get up and leave together, oblivious of the gazes of the terrified patrons.

If the worldwide reaction to *Reservoir Dogs* had been an exhilarated gasp, the response to *Pulp Fiction* was one of critics gulping back their derision. Anyone who'd predicted a damp squib, or a shallow repetition of *Dogs'* macho theatrics, had to eat their words. Tarantino had not equalled his own standards, but exceeded them.

The strength of *Pulp Fiction* (the movie of 1994, however many Oscars were won by *Forrest Gump*) lay in its abundance of hackneyed stories, stereotyped characters and general genre clichés. To try to put a new angle on them all, to make them seem born of the moment, is a career risk that could only be born by a moviemaker with near-total faith in his own abilities.

'I'm a storyteller,' says Tarantino. 'I really like experimenting with a kind of cinema that you're not used to seeing. Or taking the form and stretching it, and twisting it, and doing things that you're not used to seeing all the time.'

'I thought I was writing a crime film anthology. What Mario Bava did with the horror film in, I was going to do the same with a crime film. Then I got totally involved in the idea of going beyond that, doing what J.D. Salinger did with his Glass family stories where they're all building up to one story, characters floating in and out. It's something novelists can do because they own their characters, they can write a novel and have a lead character from three novels back show up.'

'You feel like you've seen one story about a community of characters, like *Nashville* or *Short Cuts*, where the stories are secondary. This is a much different approach – the stories are primary, not secondary, but the effect is the same.'

The initial inspiration for *Pulp Fiction* came from a 1963 movie compendium of gothic horror stories directed by Mario Bava called *Black Sabbath*. (Bava is also the name of one of the fictional brands of heroin Vincent is offered by Lance – Tarantino's most perverse tribute to date.) *Pulp Fiction* only touches briefly on the horror genre, in the Gold Watch episode, even though a long and distinguished tradition of pulp horror writing was established back in the early 1930s by *Weird Tales* magazine. In fact, the movie can take credit for putting the arcane term 'pulp fiction' back in the popular consciousness, and for making the term synonymous with pulp crime fiction.

Alain Delon in Jean-Pierre Melville's Le Samourai *(released as* The Godson *in the USA and* The Samurai *in the UK; 1967). Melville was also heavily influenced by American films noirs, and in turn was an influence on Tarantino (see chapter 4).*

The Long Goodbye *(1973): Together with Hawks'* The Big
Sleep, *Robert Altman's film is the Raymond Chandler
adaptation Tarantino most admires. However, the film is
almost as far as* Pulp Fiction *from the traditional world of
Chandler. Marlowe (Elliott Gould) is, as ever, a white
knight in a dirty world, but here he's also out of place and
time – a Jewish New Yorker among the amoral 1970s
Californian Me-Generation.*

'My stuff so far has definitely fallen into what
I consider pulp fiction,' Tarantino commented at
the time of his two-and-a-half-hour trash epic's
release. 'I think *Reservoir Dogs* fits in that. *True
Romance* fits in that. I always associate lurid
crime fiction with pulp. Mysteries fit into that,
too. If you're going to get historical, then the
whole idea of pulp, what it really means, is a paperback you don't really care about. You
read it, put it in your back pocket, sit on it in the bus, and the pages start coming out,
and who gives a fuck? When you're finished it you hand it to someone else to read, or
you throw it away. You don't put it in your library.'

'*Pulp* sneaked in through the cracks, it was made for a certain brand of reader. The
pulps weren't put under any kind of critical light except in retrospect. What's cool about
that is that's how I felt about exploitation movies in the 70s. I was going to see all these
movies and they weren't being put under any critical light, so you made your own
discoveries, you found the diamonds in the dustbin.'

Big-screen inspiration for *Pulp Fiction* came from *film noir* movies and the type of
hardboiled black and white action movie described by film critic Manny Faber as
'roughneck... faceless movies, taken from a type of half-polished trash writing... Tight,
cliché-ridden melodramas about stock musclemen.' But the hardboiled movie ethic of the
40s and 50s itself was informed by literary styles.

Much of the inspiration for *Pulp* has already been attributed by various critics to
Dashiell Hammett, who invented the hardboiled detective genre, to Raymond Chandler,
who developed it into an art form, and to James M. Cain, who set his stories of murder
and retribution not among the professional underworld, but among desperate, faithless
men and women, prepared to kill for both money and love. However, though Tarantino
has absorbed much of these writers' works throughout his formative years – two
Chandler adaptations, Hawks' *The Big Sleep* and Altman's *The Long Goodbye*, number
among his huge list of favourite movies – *Pulp Fiction* comes from somewhere more
perverse, more left-of-field.

One influence was Jim Thompson, whose tales of the deadbeat and the damned
smacked of an American gothic realism; less recognised but more in tune, perhaps, were
the macabre fatal traps set in narrative form by Cornell Woolrich, a neurotic mama's

boy whose darkest writings have been compared with Poe. Often writing under the pseudonym William Irish, Woolrich's pulp novels provided rich pickings for thriller movies, producing at least three classics in Mark Robson's eerie *The Leopard Man*, Hitchcock's claustrophobic *Rear Window*, and Claude Chabrol's brooding *The Bride Wore Black*.

Even more unsung, though his tricky plot devices resonate in *Pulp Fiction*'s manipulative framework, are the works of Fredric Brown, a pulp crime/science fiction author regarded as a 'writer's writer' by some of his contemporaries. Brown had a way of directing the reader towards the plot's anticipated conclusion, then pulling the carpet from beneath them, and his characters, by undermining the reality of all that's gone before with a final narrative quirk. (In *Pulp Fiction*, Tarantino uses this technique in reverse, diverting hellish no-exit narratives toward unforeseen happy endings.) As prolific as the best of them, Brown had the plot of his 1947 pulp, *The Screaming Mimi*, used for *The Bird with the Crystal Plumage*, the 1969 directorial debut of Dario Argento (see chapter 4).

More contemporarily, Tarantino credits internationally successful crime writer Elmore Leonard as his favourite present-day author. Leonard is the author of 33 novels, many of which are set in a low-life Florida; his conmen, bail bondsmen, thieves, dealers and killers all speak with a tarnished wit born of their creator's black humour. Several of Leonard's novels have been filmed, with varying degrees of success – *52 Pickup*, Abel Ferrara's *Cat Chaser*, *Get Shorty*, with John Travolta – and Tarantino struck a deal to obtain the screen rights to three of Leonard's titles in 1995 (see chapter 7).

Standing between the respected current-day crime writing of Leonard, and the neglected, recently rediscovered pulps, is Charles Willeford. Willeford, whose filmed titles include *Miami Blues* and *Cockfighter* (adapted from his novel *Born to Kill* by Monte Hellman, and banned in the UK for its depiction of animal-maiming sport) is a stylistic descendant of Jim Thompson, setting his stories in a black comic USA where losers play desperately to win, and the most ruthless winners kill to retain what they have. Even his roman noirs less specifically concerned with crime – like *Hungry Wives* and *High Priest of California* – dwell on the absurdities and the paranoia of modern American life: conmen capitalising on broken hearts, friendly psychopaths in the convenience store, 'Armed Response' signs on suburban front lawns.

'It's not *noir*. I don't do neo-*noir*,' insists Tarantino, emphasising how the bright crystal clarity of his pictures has little in common with *noir*'s shadowy diffusion, even if they're set in similar morally landmined territory. 'I see *Pulp Fiction* as closer to modern-day crime fiction, a little closer to Charles Willeford, though I don't know if that describes it either. What's similar is that Willeford is doing his own thing with his own characters, creating a whole environment and a whole family. The thing that is so great is that those fucking characters become so real to you that when you read each new book and you find out what's going on with his daughters and his old partner, they're almost like members of your own family. I don't think I've ever felt that way about characters in a series of books before.' (Elsewhere, Tarantino has stressed an affinity with the private universe and recurring characters of J. D. Salinger – although Salinger's not an author he returns to as frequently as Willeford or Leonard, not having the latters' gift for placing likeable lowlifes in believably dangerous situations.)

Most representative of Tarantino's regard for crime fiction is Tim Roth and Amanda Plummer's early conversation about the difficulty of pulling hold-ups. 'We keep on, one of those gook motherfucker's gonna make us kill 'em,' complains Pumpkin (Roth) of the hassle with oriental family stores. The sentiment is straight out of Eddie Bunker's *No Beast So Fierce* (see chapter 2).

The prologue

The coffee shop setting which opens and closes the movie is an LA milieu Tarantino easily identifies with. Even when he and his video geek buddies couldn't afford to buy dinner, there was always a late night coffee shop where they could hang out over a single capuccino.

'My friends and I would go to coffee shops late at night and be there for hours,' he recalls, 'like our version of hanging out in a Parisian cafe and discussing existentialism, except we were talking about New World Pictures and whether we were ever going to be with a woman.'

Into this everyday setting come a pair of stick-up artists, played by Tim Roth and Amanda Plummer. Roth, Tarantino's rat-faced regular, is allowed to drop *Dogs'* fake Californian drawl in favour of his native South London tones, while Plummer talks in tones reminiscent of the fractured, nicotine-stained upper-middle classness of a Marianne Faithfull.

Honey Bunny (Amanda Plummer) starts to freak as the coffee shop hold-up gets out of control.

'Some parts I wrote especially for certain people,' says Tarantino. 'I wrote the Wolf for Harvey Keitel. I wrote the English outlaws Pumpkin and Honey Bunny for Tim Roth and Amanda Plummer. I saw them once together and it was a director's moment: I've got to put these two together in a movie. I could have been seduced by the idea of casting Tim in the Vincent role when Michael Madsen dropped out because he would have done wonders with it, but I had so much written Pumpkin and Honey Bunny for Tim and Amanda that I would never be able to get into the roles without them.'

Pumpkin and Honey Bunny's good-thief-bad-thief routine, as they rob the diner, also provides the alert viewer with a continuity quirk along the lines of the Who-Shot-Nice-Guy-Eddie? discrepancy in *Dogs*. 'Any one of you fuckin' pricks move and I'll execute every motherfuckin' one of you!' screams the hyper Honey Bunny (Plummer) in the Prologue. In the Epilogue at the end of the narrative time loop, the replay of this scene has her screaming, 'Any one of you fuckin' pricks move and I'll execute every one of you motherfuckers!' The inconsistency originates in the script, remaining in the published version – it's so obvious on a second viewing that it can only be Tarantino playing tantalising games with his audience again. (If it wasn't intentional, surely the same piece of footage would simply have been used twice.)

The post-credits entrance of Jules (Samuel L. Jackson) and Vincent (John Travolta) is by now one of the best remembered (and most parodied) moments in modern cinema. Hash, cheeseburgers, foot massages are all debated by the two killers in the Chevrolet as if they don't have a care in the world. And most likely they don't. They're on the way to a hit, but there's little sense of anticipated trouble; not even the intensity of the six reservoir dogs strutting their way from the coffeehouse. That aside, Jules and Vincent still look like a couple of refugees from *Dogs*. Black bargain-rack suit, white shirt, black Slim Jim tie, they have the trademark look.

'When Jean-Pierre Melville was making his crime films, he talked about how it was very important that his characters have a suit of armour,' explains Tarantino. 'His was the snap-brim fedora and Bogart-like trenchcoat. Leone had the dusters, Eastwood the poncho. I've always said the mark of any good action film is that when you get through seeing it, you want to dress like the character. That's totally the case, for instance, with Chow Yun-Fat's wardrobe in the *A Better Tomorrow* movies [directed by John Woo – see chapter 4]. The black suits in *Pulp Fiction*, that's my suit of armour.'

Clothes are also used as a continuity signpost. At the beginning of the first story proper, 'Vincent Vega and Marsellus Wallace's Wife', Jules and Vincent come schlepping into a downtown bar owned by Marsellus dressed like dorks in shorts, baseball cap and t-shirts. 'Goddamn nigger, what's up with them clothes?' asks the barman, taken back by the sight.

'When you first see Vincent and Jules, their suits are cut and crisp, they look like real bad-asses,' remarks Tarantino, explaining his dramatic sleight-of-hand. 'But as the movie goes on, their suits get more and more fucked up up until they're stripped off and the two are dressed in the exact antithesis – volley ball wear, which is not cool.'

By the end of the third story, 'The Bonnie Situation', the suits have been sprayed by blood and gore. Their makeshift apparel is taken from the wardrobe of Jimmie (Tarantino himself), the obliging but nervous friend Jules drops in on when he wants to dispose of a corpse. These are the clothes Jules and Vincent are seen wearing at the beginning of the first story, which means the 'real-time' chronology of the three stories and the linking episode runs like this: first, 'The Bonnie Situation' (Story Three); second, the interlinking Prologue and Epilogue, set during the diner robbery; third,'Vincent Vega and Marsellus's Wife' (Story One); fourth and last, 'The Gold Watch' (Story Two).

This enables the author to play the movie's celebrated quirk, whereby Vincent, who we see blown unceremoniously away in a toilet during Story Two, returns to provide the movie's splattery faux pas in Story Three and to stride nonchalantly away from the coffee shop with Jules in the Epilogue. By implication, the retirement of Jules from 'the Life' – his resolution to retire taking place in the epilogue – results in the blunder which leaves Vincent shot to pieces in Story Two. Somehow, if his superbad-superspade partner was around, you can't imagine him allowing Vincent to get sloppy enough to go take a crap while leaving his submachine gun on the kitchen unit.

The movie's second intentional discrepancy also comes courtesy of Jules: when he and Vincent finish blasting the yuppie hoods in the Prologue, his .45 is locked back in the open position, showing he's out of bullets. When the scene replays later in 'The Bonnie Situation' the slide is forward and the gun remains loaded after firing, allowing him to blow away the hidden gunman who's 'miraculously' missed with every shot. (In the same scene, a bullethole appears in the wall behind Jules' shoulder a moment before we hear the gunman from the toilet open up on him, but this seems more like an old-fashioned continuity error.)

However likeable Travolta's gloriously fucked-up and gracelessly charming Vincent is, Samuel L. Jackson's Jules remains the Mr Superbad of the partnership. As stone-cold hired assassins go, he's a hero. His roots are in the 'shoot-first-and-jivetalk-later' blaxploitation thrillers of the 1970s. So is his hair – his jheri-curls ('processed' afro hair cut to shape and held by gallons of coconut oil) are the style of the 70s, celebrated in the 90s.

'That happened by mistake,' testifies Tarantino. 'I've always liked afros – if I were black, I'd wear an afro. I talked to Sam about wearing an afro [Jackson has close-cut hair and normally goes without a moustache] and he was up for that. The make-up woman went out to get some afro wigs, but because she didn't know the difference she also showed up with the jheri-curl wig. Sam put it on, and it was great. It was Jules.'

Samuel Jackson testifies to the novelty of his character's dialogue: 'I sat down, read the script straight through, which I normally don't do, took a breath, then read it again, which I never do, just to make sure it was true. That it was the best script I'd ever read... When people see killers for hire, they tend to think that they sit at home, they clean their guns, they sharpen their knives, they polish their bullets and all these other things. But Quentin takes you into a world where you actually find out that they gossip. They talk

Pulp Fiction: *Vincent and Jules (Samuel L. Jackson) stop the chat and get down to business with Brett and his cronies.*

about their lives outside of what they do. He has a facility for creating everyday language and sensibilities for his characters.'

As Mia later complains to Vincent, these hoods spend their time 'gossiping like some sewing circle'. On their way to shooting the gang of boys Jules and Vincent bullshit about the borderline legality of hashish in Amsterdam; what cheeseburgers are called in France; whether a foot massage is an erotic act or not – engrossing themselves in a controversy over whether Tony Rocky Horror, some hoodlum friend of theirs, deserved to be flung over a balcony for caressing Marsellus' wife's foot. Tarantino makes the point that the killings are just another day's work – and who the hell wants to talk shop all the time?

'Everything I write is extremely personal and has to do with whatever is going on with me at that moment,' testifies Tarantino. 'I was experiencing Europe for the first time when I wrote *Pulp Fiction*, thus John Travolta's character has just come back from Europe and that's all he can talk about.'

Tarantino's disinclination to flog a gimmick to death ensures that once the hitmen get inside the criminal brats' apartment, Jules drops the naturalistic patter and comes on like an avenging angel. 'I will strike down upon thee with great vengeance and furious anger those who attempt to poison or destroy my brothers,' he declaims, quoting from *Ezekiel*, chapter 25, verse 17. He sounds for all the world like Preacher Harry Powell, the murderous man of God played by Robert Mitchum in *The Night of the Hunter*, the

Southern Gothic masterpiece directed by Charles Laughton. Tarantino, however, credits Sonny Chiba, the Japanese karate star, with inspiration, pointing out how the enemies in his TV series, Shadow Warriors, would always face a verbose morality lecture before being dispatched from this world.

Tarantino credited Tony Scott, director of *True Romance* for influencing *Pulp Fiction*. Scott's camera style is alien to most of Tarantino's work so far, which normally dwells on central figures and confined spaces, all shot with unorthodox angles and massive close-ups. But the immediate post-credits section of *Pulp* follows Scott's action style of rapid-cutting, with one cut every 15 seconds.'

'John and Sam Jackson were so electric together that I actually considered making a whole bunch of Vincent and Jules movies, kind of like *The Continuing Adventures of...*,' Tarantino admits, though he's cagey about being tied down any kind of *Pulp Fiction* 2 project.

'I like the idea that I'm taking a genre that already exists and reinventing it, like Leone re-invented the whole Western genre. I think I've taken on an established genre like the pulp thriller and made it challenging to myself and to my audience.'

'The idea was to use these really old stories – you know, the boxer who's supposed to throw the fight and doesn't, the dangerous love triangle between this guy and his boss's wife, some gangsters trying to get rid of a body – the sort of thing you've seen a zillion times before. I want to take these genre characters and put them in a real-life situation.'

Vincent Vega and Marsellus Wallace's wife

The Jack Rabbit Slim's set in the 'Vincent Vega and Marsellus Wallace's Wife' sequence was built for $150,000. (This is knockdown budgeting – original estimates, for a more solidly-founded set, came to $500,000. But, as the director realised, solidity doesn't count for much when the camera lies so well.) Decorated with posters for B-movies such as *Shock Confessions of a Sorority Girl* and *Attack of the 50-Foot Woman*, the place is a monument to kitschy 50s trash culture.

'Every big city has a couple of them, these 50s retro restaurants. I don't like them that much, to me they are always trying too hard,' says Tarantino, surprisingly, given his anti-snobbish love of pop culture's more cheap and cheerful aspects. 'In fact, the script even says, "Either the best or the worst of these places, depending on your point of view." This one is a cross between the 50s restaurants that exist, the nightclub where Elvis Presley and the car racers hang out in *Speedway*, and the bar where all the racecar drivers hang out in Howard Hawks' *Red Line 7000*. The thing that makes it work is the racing-car motif. The dance floor is done like a speedometer.'

Icons of the time are impersonated by the MC – Ed Sullivan – and by waiters dressed up as Marilyn Monroe and Buddy Holly. (The latter is a walk-on role for Steve Buscemi, as a waiter depressed by his career as a lookalike for the great rockabilly dork. 'I think Quentin should do a cutaway to show that I don't get a tip,' deadpanned Buscemi on set.) Even the orders come with a vintage celebrity bias: you can have a

*Left: (*Shock Confessions of a) Sorority Girl *(1957). Pretty lame attempt by Roger Corman to transfer the juvenile delinquent genre into a more middle-class setting. The poster appears in the Jack Rabbit Slim's sequences of* Pulp Fiction *(along with other 50s Corman movies);* Pulp *also featured an appearance by Corman regular Dick Miller as breaking-yard owner Monster Joe.*

Vincent and Uma in their fifties' car body table at Jack Rabbit Slim's.

Martin and Lewis or Amos and Andy shake, to accompany your Douglas Sirk steak, which – fittingly, for the director of *Magnificent Obsession* and other overwrought melodramas – comes 'burnt to a crisp or bloody as hell'.

Sally Menke, the film editor on *Pulp Fiction*, comments that 'the idea behind this scene was that basically Quentin wanted it to be as drawn out as possible, as it would be if you were meeting someone for the first time, and you're a little bit awkward, because you don't have anything to talk about.'

'I like the idea that the whole thing is about a date,' enthuses Tarantino, 'a date, a date, a date, he's going on a date with Mia Wallace! – and when they get there, you have a date, you're with them. They don't just go – gibberish – bullshit – "Oh you too?" – "Right" – "Let's go!" And then they split. I like the fact that you actually hang out with them, that you get to know Mia, and you get to know Vincent via Mia, through the course of the time that they're together.'

'There's a lot of dialogue that's been taken out of the scene,' explains Sally Menke. 'I actually lobbied hard to take out even more dialogue, and Quentin really stuck by his guns and wanted it to remain as long as it is. Especially the silences, where they're not talking at all.'

'I don't find it boring at all,' responds Tarantino, 'I enjoy it. And also, I think you get totally more involved with them, so after that, when the story takes off, it means so much more, and it actually makes things move even faster. My point of view is, if you're afraid of talking then you shouldn't be watching one of my movies.'

Despite the clichéd, lazy Mr Guns an' Guts label, Tarantino's crime movies are of little interest to anyone who isn't keen to watch the genre being subverted. Watching careful characterisations and archetypes dance within inches of each other, firing off more verbal sparks than torso-bursting bullets, counts for most of the fun. It's not for everyone – Ken Russell, for one: Britain's elder statesman of operatic scale excess, couldn't appreciate the outrageous liberties taken in *Pulp Fiction*. 'It was very slow,' he claims, having left the cinema with his wife after less than an hour.

'I don't think my films are hard to follow,' Tarantino counters. 'The only thing that's required is that you have to commit to watching them, you have to engage with them totally. I don't make films for the casual viewer.'

That said his movies, however, are not mere 'talkfests' with the odd spot of blood. First and foremost, they're entertainment, designed with the most movie-literate audience in mind: himself. Pulp's major progression on *Dogs* is that all the requisite elements for having fun were present this time: cool dialogue, violence, sex, horror, comedy, music – even song and dance.

Pop culture is obviously celebrated like it's going out of fashion – but, unlike the overkill of *True Romance*, it's a little more implicit, more contained in the cinematic context. The whole Jack Rabbit Slim's episode is a celebration of 50s nostalgia, no matter how its creator feels about 'theme restaurants'. Vincent – who tells Jules he never watches TV – is enough of a 50s-hip 'Elvis man' to tell Marilyn from Mamie Van Doren, starlet of 50s exploitation epics like *High School Confidential*, and to note the absence of *The Girl Can't Help It* star Jayne Mansfield.

Other aspects: burgers are more celebrated here than anywhere outside a McDonald's ad or a *Popeye* cartoon, whether they're 'Royales with cheese' or 'Big Kahuna burgers' (the latter seem to be inventions, to avoid further accusations of product placement – as with the 'Red Apples' brand of cigarettes). Jules calls one of the Yuppie crooks 'Flock of Seagulls', his hairstyle calling to mind a lame early-80s Brit 'new romantic' band, who no-one – least of all a black gunman – would normally admit to remembering. Mia uses 'disco' as a euphemism for 'hot' and an all-purpose exclamation; she also describes the all-girl group of super agents from the TV pilot she starred in, *Fox Force Five*, thus '[the blonde one] had a photographic memory, the Japanese fox was a kung fu master, the black girl was a demolition expert, the French fox's speciality was sex...' Besides the resemblance to *Charlie's Angels*, this is more redolent of Ted V. Mikels' low-budget 1973 movie *The Doll Squad*, featuring a squad of six chicks with a host of skills including karate, pathology, and an ingenious use of weapons by group leader Sabrina (same name as the *Charlie's Angels* leader, but three years before), such as lethal cigarette lighters and 'mace-rings'. As Butch and Fabienne get ready to leave the hotel room in the morning, she's watching *The Losers* on TV, a 1970 AIP flick in which a bike gang, including celebrated character actor William

Every Which Way But Loose Smith, take on the Vietcong army. Before Vincent is blasted down Butch spots him leaving the john with a copy of *Modesty Blaise*, a piece of 60s pulp about a femme fatale version of James Bond (he's reading it on the john in the diner hold-up epilogue, which means he's either a very slow reader or his end is nigh). While Fabby's waiting for her white knight to carry her away on Zed's chopper, she's wearing a 'Frankie says Relax' t-shirt. When Vincent tries to convince Jules their escape is not a miracle, he cites a similar instance on the American Mondo TV series, *Cops*. When the Wolf lightens up after disposing of the blood-stained car, he grabs Jules' wrist and jokingly intones 'It's your future. I see ...a cab ride,' like the psychic played by Christopher Walken in *The Dead Zone*. When Jules is putting Pumpkin, the stick-up artist, in his place, he refers to him as 'Ringo', one of Tarantino's favourite spaghetti western characters. Jules tries to cool the dangerously neurotic Honey Bunny down and get her finger off the trigger by asking, 'What is Fonzie?', her answer earning the Fonzie-esque response, 'Correctamundo'.

Ultimately, Jules swears to Vincent he's forsaking the Life to 'walk the earth...like Caine in Kung Fu'. This earns the materialist's derision – to him, David Carradine's poor-but-holy, battling Shaolin monk signifies nothing but a sorry-ass bum.

As with *Romance* some references didn't make it past script stage, though here the number's less excessive: Vincent and Jules' original approach to the yuppie brats' apartment specifies they should wear matching overcoats, almost dragging along the ground (pure Leone – *Once Upon a Time in the West*); when Vincent originally entered Mia's apartment, she was to take time to quiz him over whether he was an Elvis or a Beatles man, to make him choose between favourite trash TV shows – *Bewitched* or *I Dream of Jeannie*, *The Brady Bunch* or *The Partridge Family*; the obsession with the Partridges getting just a little tiresome – more intriguingly, when quizzed whether he's ever fantasised about being beaten up by a girl, he says Emma Peel of *The Avengers*.

Music was especially pivotal in the movie's acceptance as a piece of well-crafted fun, overriding all the pontification about neo-*noir*. As with *Dogs*, a broad selection of AM radio hits – from funk, and blue-eyed soul, to trebly guitar rock – plays along against the action, never letting us forget it's taking place deep in the world of pop culture. Unlike *Dogs* much of the music is of a type – guitar-based, early 60s American rock, heavy on the tremolo. Forgotten guitar heroes electrify the soundtrack, like Link Wray, with his 'Rumble' – an instrumental rock'n'roll evocation of a gang fight, sometimes credited as the first heavy metal record. Most recognisable is 'Misirlou', by Dick Dale, the vibrato stand-out of a batch of surf-rock instrumentals, its use during the opening credits labelling it forever as 'the *Pulp Fiction* music'.

'I'm using surf music as the basic score – from the 60s, Dick Dale style,' Tarantino explained at the time of release. 'I don't understand the surfer connection to surf music. To me surf music seems like rock 'n' roll Ennio Morricone music, rock 'n' roll spaghetti western music, that's what it sounds like. That's the basic score that – along with the songs that are played – runs throughout the film.'

Would-be gangsters become impromptu hoofers: the dance sequence in Jean-Luc Godard's lyrical story of alienated criminality, Bande à Part *(1964).*

'Misirlou' has become ubiquitous since the success of *Pulp Fiction* – ads, trailers, and, of course, as a semi-orchestral arrangement for Tarantino and Avary to ascend the steps at the 1995 Oscar ceremony. Dick Dale – formerly a little-known electric guitar innovator whose left-handed style is said to have influenced Jimi Hendrix, and who once played on the same bill in Little Richard's backing band – had spent years as a record company executive before returning to performing and recording. Although he had never played a concert outside Southern California before his mid-50s, the success of the movie saw him travelling to North London for gigs in front of a 20-something grunge-rock crowd.

The other soundtrack highlight of the movie is another guitar-rock number, but a more contemporary recording. 'The big song, the one that is so fucking vivid,' says Tarantino, 'is Urge Overkill's version of Neil Diamond's "Girl Who'll Be a Woman Soon", which is what the boss's wife Mia is dancing to when she snorts the heroin and has her OD.'

Its vividness is contained in the set piece, where the song's moody lustfulness makes a perfect counterpoint to the blackly funny on-screen action. The most effective piece of music – rather than the most affecting soundtrack contribution – comes in the sequence where Mia and Vincent dance to Chuck Berry's 'You Never Can Tell'. The song itself is just a rhythm, drowned in the action – this ain't just rock 'n' roll, this is song and dance.

'I always love the musical sequences in movies, and I particularly love them when the movies aren't musicals,' Tarantino explains. 'My favourite musical sequences have always been in Godard, because they just come out of nowhere. It's so infectious, so friendly. And the fact that it's not a musical, but he's stopping the movie to have a musical sequence, makes it all the more sweet.'

So the blueprint for Pulp's wacky dance contest number, with Mia (Uma Thurman) and Vincent doing the Twist with infectious enthusiasm and, in Vincent's case, little coordination, came not from *The Girl Can't Help It* or *Grease*, but from the ironic auteur of 'critical cinema'.

'Uma is not the kind of person to just hit the dance floor with everyone watching her,' Tarantino recalls with amused affection. 'That's just not her. She was nervous about doing the dance, because she thought she had to dance. She thought she had to be good because I'm having a big scene and we're stopping to show the dance. We're having a dance number. But then what we did, on the day of the shoot – I talked to her about the Twist, and we practised it together, and we all worked it out a little bit during rehearsal. But then, I waited for the day of the dance, the dancing, and by then it was the last day we were in Jack Rabbit Slim's. What I did was, I got her and John together in the trailer and I showed them the dance scene from *Bande À Part*. And I go: "They're not dancers. They're not executing a dance perfectly. But for my money they're the greatest dancers in the world. They're having fun. They're not dancing well, but they're actually dancing great. Because they're having fun, and I'm enjoying watching them enjoying doing the dance. That's what I want you to do." And they both got it! Once they saw that: "Okay, I know exactly what you want. Let's do it."'

'Whenever I'd see those scenes in a Godard movie, it made me wish I had a rewind facility in the cinema. Sometimes they almost ruin the movie, because you love them so much, you want to go over it again and again. In *Le Petit Soldat*, when she's doing the interview, taking her pictures, and all of a sudden she puts on some classical music and dances around the room. When she takes the music off, you're like, "Oh, it's over." I learned that for this film, don't let it linger.'

In tribute to Godard's urbane take on the modern outlaw film, Tarantino has named his own production company A Band Apart – signified by the silhouettes of his *Reservoir Dogs*, the ultimate band of outsiders.

Mia Wallace is the first female character of Tarantino's to hit the screen who, while being essentially an archetype, is somewhere nearly as idiosyncratic and well-drawn as the men. Alabama Whitman may have been appealing, but she's equal parts cutesy pie, best-buddy wish-fulfillment and wet dream. Mia comes on like a coked-up vamp, but her sense of fun, her understated interest in Vincent, her wry sense of humour – 'that's a little more information than I need, but go ahead,' she tells him when he announces he needs to piss – and of course Uma Thurman's natural beauty, topped with a wilder version of the Louise Brooks bob, make for a most prepossessing two-dimensional sex object. Up till the smack overdose, that is.

Casting was all-important – despite the several major film actresses considered for the part (including Meg Ryan and Holly Hunter), Uma Thurman is so natural as Mia that an alternative seems inconceivable. At the time of casting, Tarantino claimed he knew everything about his main female character apart from what she looked like. On meeting the pulchritudinous model-turned-actress (whose lips one journalist has described as 'so plump you could land a helicopter on them'), Tarantino was convinced he'd found Mia Wallace. Briefly married to Tim Roth's South London pal and now American movie star Gary Oldman, she made her first notable appearance naked inside an oyster shell, in Terry Gilliam's *The Adventures of Baron Munchausen*, followed by character roles including one of John Malkovich's seducees in *Dangerous Liaisons*, and alongside DeNiro and Bill Murray in *Mad Dog and Glory*, the neglected crime comedy by director John McNaughton. It took the glamorous 24-year-old a little persuasion to agree to a part where she's called to graphically overdose. Ultimately, she was won over by Tarantino himself, or by, as she describes it: 'His personality and his passion, his enthusiasm for filmmaking, a heart behind it and a sincerity with which he conducts himself, which unfortunately is not a run-of-the-mill quality.'

'If I have a problem, it's that there are so many actors I want to work with and I don't feel I'm going to have time to work with them all,' admits Tarantino, still the unashamed fan. 'So I try to take care of as many as I can in the course of one movie. The casting is really important to me. I'm knocked out by the performances everybody has given. I didn't want some star-studded bullshit – they've got real characters and when they came in they had to come to play.'

'Travolta is a truly great actor. *Blow Out* is one of my all-time favourite films. Everybody seems to forget that around the time of *Saturday Night Fever*, he was being touted as the next Pacino – you know, Oscar-nominated, and he deserved it.'

Tarantino's first meeting with Travolta was at what had been the latter's LA apartment, but which was now rented by Tarantino himself. Unphased by the venue, the former superstar made it through the social niceties, only to be hit by a tirade from the director: 'Don't you remember what Pauline Kael said about you? What Truffaut said about you? What Bertolucci said about you? Don't you know what you mean to the American cinema? John, what did you do?'

Travolta admitted to being 'hurt – but moved'. The spiel was intended to bully him into accepting the part of Vincent Vega, the recognition of a prime role not being Travolta's great talent. (In the late 70s and early 80s he turned down the leads in *Midnight Express*, *American Gigolo* and *Prince of the City*.) Tarantino had apparently become so set on casting Travolta that he issued an ultimatum to the studio: 'You either do it with John Travolta or you don't do it.'

Travolta himself almost added it to his roster of great missed opportunities, as he regarded Vincent as a negative role model. Apparently, he believed any success for the movie might help turn 90s kids into wannabe-assassins with smack habits, much as he

John Travolta in Blow Out *(1981): 'One of the very best American film actors around. He was awesome in De Palma's* Blow Out*. I used to watch that film over and over and wonder why other directors weren't using him.' Basically an audio-based take on Antonioni's 'swinging London' story of a murder hidden within a photograph,* Blow Up*, the film received a cold reception on release and has remained seriously undervalued ever since. Not by Tarantino, however, who rates it among his three favourite movies.*

once had 70s jocks trying to perfect a Stayin' Alive strut and throwing their white disco jackets gracefully into the air. (Travolta almost turned down the role he was offered in the wake of *Pulp Fiction* too – Chilli Palmer, loanshark and would-be movie-maker, in the screen adaptation of Elmore Leonard's *Get Shorty*. Tarantino had to phone to put him straight on that count: 'This is not the one you say no to. This is the one you say yes to. I'm not going to let you make this mistake.')

Travolta didn't see the irony in Vincent trying to be such a stand-up dude (albeit in his own vicious world), while remaining so resolutely fucked-up. And there lies the secret of John Travolta's screen rebirth – Vincent is such a travesty of near-coolness, an outlaw role built to suit a dissipated career casualty. (Metaphorically speaking, as Travolta's career was ending up in the toilet, just like the finale to Vincent's criminal career, with *Look Who's Talking 3* the only work option in sight.) Vincent may have briefly tickled Mia Wallace's curiosity bone, but Tony Manero on the dance floor he ain't.

By the time of the movie's success and the accolades that came with it, Travolta was getting the point: '*Saturday Night Fever* was pop culture. This film is a reflection of pop culture. And that is a very big difference.' Tarantino had taken everyone offguard by recruiting a household name for the role, long written off as a lightweight has-been. The part itself is almost the antithesis of everything the former star ever stood for, but the director forged enough links between the actor and his character's debased masculinity, and a star is reborn.

'People find John Travolta's character in *Pulp Fiction* not only very likeable but very charming – considering the fact that he's first presented as a hitman and that's never taken back. He is what he is, he is shown plying his trade but then you get to know him above and beyond that. The reverse of never breaking that hitman mode in Hollywood movies is, "Wow, he can't fucking do that, he can't kill the villain with his bare hands, why don't we have him punch him and have the villain fall on something – so then he killed him but he didn't really mean to so he can go back to his family and everything is cool, we can still feel good about liking him." That kind of bullshit I can't abide.'

'Tristar were originally gonna distribute *Pulp Fiction*, but they had big problems with the scene where John Travolta's character shoots up heroin. I'm going, "Look guys, relax, it's going to be funny," and they're saying, "No, Quentin, heroin is not funny. A guy sticking a needle in his arm does not make for big laughs." In the end I just said, "You're gonna have to trust me on this one, guys." They didn't. I guess they just couldn't make the leap.'

The gross-out elements of *Pulp Fiction* are few and far between, with less gore per reel than even the surprisingly unviolent *Reservoir Dogs*. ('Only 2.5 minutes of violence,' points out Pulp's creator, and these consist of what Anne Billson refers to as 'globs' in the second *Shock Xpress* book – brief, shocking scenes of ultra-violence in an otherwise non-violent movie.) The most violent scene in the script – the accidental shooting of Marvin through the throat, followed by Vincent finishing him off while Jules honks the horn and Marvin gurgles for mercy – was moderated to Vincent blowing the boy to hell in one shot. Moreover, Tarantino decided not to show the exploding head built by the FX men (just the blood and cerebral tissue flying eveywhere), still wary of offending audience sensibilities. So much for 'the world's most violent filmmaker'.

Once the globs come, however, they're memorably visceral, resonating through the long stretches of sardonic dialogue that surround them: male gang rape; car upholstery and hairdos sprayed with arterial blood and brain tissue; most of all, in the resurrection of the OD'd Mia Wallace – with the whites of her eyes rolling, and her mouth dripping with foam and liquid vomit – the hypodermic of adrenalin thumped through the breastplate like the resurrection of a female zombie in some sicko splatter epic.

As for the LA lowlife milieu wherein Mia gets her drugs mixed and fucks herself up almost terminally, Tarantino seems mildly cognizant of it. The dealer who supplies Vincent with the 'madman' heroin has been compared with Zed, the character also played by Eric Stoltz in Avary's *Killing Zoe*; in truth, they're not much alike, apart from the long hair, beard and use of heroin. Zed is a fatalistic drifter, too unsure of his own position to turn down the offer of trying smack; Lance, the character in *Pulp* (notice that name again, a Tarantino standard in tribute to his former employer at Video Archives), is a laid-back hedonist who lives a life of stoned, sleazy matrimony with his wacko wife in suburban LA, because that's the way he likes it and you can't imagine guys like him any other way.

'Lance is a totally LA type,' says Tarantino, 'he's your friendly drug dealer. Margaret Cho did a hysterical stand-up routine about the problem with going out and buying drugs. You have to feign a relationship with the drug dealer, like you're not going over to buy pot, you're going on a social visit and drugs are incidental. You have to sit down and talk about things, as opposed to here's the money, give me my shit, let me get out of here.'

Tarantino changes tack – making the jump from the drug that's demonised by governments and used by nearly everyone, to the drug that's demonised by everyone but used by more people than seems feasible: 'Mia doesn't do too well by drugs. One journalist told me I could show that whole first scene of her overdose to schoolkids as an anti-drug movie. People ask me where I came up with the story about the overdose: the bottom line is that every junkie, or person who has experimented seriously with heroin, has a version of that story – they almost died, someone else almost died and they brought them back with salt water, or put them in a tub, or jumped them with a car battery.'

Tarantino clearly had great fun playing with the one taboo that can outrage moralists, politicians and columnists even more than screen violence – the evil of drugs. As he describes the effect of Mia Wallace's OD resurrection: 'Like a third of the audience is diving under the chairs, and another third is laughing hysterically, and the other third is doing both at the same time... I don't know why this is so funny, but...'

'Violence entertains Quentin,' says Travolta, loyally making a pre-emptive defence, 'but that is not part of his life. It's not like he's working out demons. He is just working out all the stuff that entertained him growing up. Quentin is one of the sweetest people you have ever met. He has a huge heart.'

The gold watch

Roger Avary's contributory episode of *Pulp Fiction* (originally entitled '*Pandemonium Reigns*') was, claims Tarantino, largely rewritten to match the fabric of all that goes on around it: 'There is only one scene in the film that is pure Roger,' he says. 'It is the scene in the bathroom where Bruce explains everything that he's going to do [reassuring Fabienne – Maria de Madeiros – that they'll have enough money to fly off to the South Pacific and 'live like hogs in the fat house forever']. I love that scene. I suppose that he has little lines interspersed throughout the story. [Or little scenes, according to Avary.] But the only full-on Roger scene is that one.'

Tarantino takes credit for the more effective bedroom scene beforehand, where Butch, stripped of his callous tough-guy attitude, implicitly reveals how Fabienne is the only person in the world he could ever treat tenderly.

'The perspective outside the doorway during the scene between Bruce and Maria...is set up that way so you feel like you're a fly on the wall, observing these people alone together,' says Tarantino, 'acting like people act when they're alone. The sequence when they're in the hotel room, it should be somewhat uncomfortable and embarrassing being in the room with them because they're madly in love with each other and they're at that uppermost honeymoon point of a relationship so they're talking all this babytalk. You're watching something you shouldn't really be seeing, and you don't know how much you want to see it because there's an extreme level of intimacy going on.'

Tarantino also claims another major addition to the original blueprint: 'In Roger Avary's original story the fact that Butch had a gold watch came out of nowhere. Roger spent all this time trying to sell us on why Butch had to go back into danger, and he did a really good job, but he didn't quite sell it. I thought, well, it's a contrivance, and what you do with a plot contrivance is feature it.'

The beginning of the 'The Gold Watch' sequence not only parodies Walken's role in *The Deer Hunter* – as a traumatised Nicky, long-term Viet Cong POW held in a wooden cage, eventually throwing his life away in an existential game of Russian Roulette – but the whole war movie genre. As Walken says: '*The Deer Hunter* had nothing to do with Vietnam, it had to do with young men going to war thinking that it's adventurous and getting their legs blown off.' In fact, the enforced games of Russian Roulette inflicted by the VCs on their prisoners were the invention of director Cimino, and had only the faintest anecdotal connection with the Vietnam War. In *The Deer Hunter*, Cimino was

The Deer Hunter *(1978), Michael Cimino's investigation of war heroism and Hollywood's falsification of it, a film deliberately echoed by the Gold Watch sequence of* Pulp Fiction.

tackling the big macho themes of patriotism, honour in the face of fear and death, bravery and loyalty – in a style respectfully devoid of mockery but laced with the tragic. Similarly, so did Tarantino in 'The Gold Watch' – we may laugh at the intensity of Walken's dedication to his vow of bringing that watch home to little Butch, but we're being encouraged to laugh (with affection) at the way Hollywood portrays such ordeals of honour – not at honour itself.

Further rationale for the sequence came from the director's thrill at having Walken on board, albeit only for a short cameo. 'You can write a three-page monologue and "good luck" on having someone deliver it perfectly,' says Tarantino. 'Chris Walken is one of those actors who can and rarely gets the opportunity to do so. I called him up and said, "Chris, I have a three-page monologue for you and I promise I won't cut a word." We planned to do it on the last day of shooting: when he came in I told him he had all day, we're not going to leave until we get it right.'

Part of the fun of *Pulp Fiction* is how it does not only play subversive games with a cherished movie genre, but with two household names. John Travolta, meet Bruce Willis. Vincent, meet Butch.

'I love that scene,' enthuses Tarantino of the two characters' brief barroom meeting. With Vincent sneering out the side of his mouth at the 'punchy palooka', the dialogue sounds like 'it's straight out of *On The Waterfront*. It's a true... movie star... moment. It's like really kinda cool. It's like wow! God! A couple of movie stars! And what's funny about it is: there's no reason why the two characters don't like each other. They just don't. It's like the two leads in a movie and you can't even put them in the same frame without getting on each other's nerves – it's like two dogs walking down the street: "Grrr."'

Much as it looks like the Bruce Willis episode is going to be the old one-man-and-his-two-fists-against-the-mob routine, Tarantino has stranger fish to fry: 'Part of the fun in *Pulp*, like in the middle story with Bruce Willis, is that if you're hip to movies, you're watching the boxing movie *Body and Soul* and then suddenly the characters turn a corner and they're in the middle of *Deliverance*. And you're like, "What? How did I get into *Deliverance*? I was in Body and Soul, what's going on here? I turn a corner and I'm in the middle of *Deliverance* – *Deliverance* already in progress. How did that happen?" Now if you're not into those movies, then you're just following what happens to Bruce's character, Butch. It's the same response, except there's no movie reference; it's just like "How did we go from the frying pan into this fire?"'

One direct movie reference comes in the scene where Butch drives off from his apartment, after blowing Vincent away, and makes brief eye contact with Marsellus who is crossing the road. Before kissing asphalt, Marsellus turns to the driver with a half-conscious look of recognition, just like Janet Leigh's boss, from whom she's stolen a lot of money, in Hitchcock's *Psycho*. Butch has pulled a different double cross, but is in even deeper shit. The accusatory gaze through the windshield, as in *Psycho*, is the last glimmer of a suffocating reality the driver wants to escape. But a short detour takes Butch (and Marsellus) somewhere much worse. Just as Janet Leigh wound up in a motel run by a necrophiliac, so the hunter and the hunted fall into Zed and Maynard's hell-on-earth pawnshop.

As well as being nightmare territory, the pawnshop sequence has a sadistic slapstick feel. The sudden deviation goes some way beyond the Body and Soul/*Deliverance* switch; almost surreal, it negates any claim to hardboiled realism. One minute, it seems, we're watching a Tarantino movie, the next minute it's taken over by one of the sleazy Euro-exploitation moviemakers he admires – who's decided to throw in some sexual sadism, regardless of context.

Tarantino's inescapably wide frame of movie reference contextualises everything he does. At the beginning of the take for the scene which ends with Butch leaving the pawnshop triumphant, the director hollered at Willis: 'This is it! The camera's right on you. You're Robert Mitchum in *Thunder Road*.' But, as his own explanation shows, the character of Butch encapsulates a whole backlog of screen hero memories.

'He's gonna be a hero when he goes back out. He would have been completely justified, all right, to just walk out the door, after what's happened. But he decides that whatever this guy has done, he can't leave him to it, that's a fate that not even Marsellus deserves. So he's gonna go back in there and he's gonna do something about it. He's gonna be a hero, that's a very heroic moment.

'But now he's gotta find something in this pawn shop to go and attack these guys with, so he picks up a hammer, and he thinks about that, then he picks up a baseball bat, then he picks up a chainsaw, and he finally settles on a samurai sword. And it's almost like, OK, I'm going to be a hero, which hero am I going to be? Who am I gonna walk through the door as? He picks up the hammer because that's almost realistic, that's almost like him, because you hear a burglar downstairs and you pick up some implement that comes to hand – that's normal. But then he picks up the baseball bat and it's like he's gonna be Joe Don Baker as Buford Pusser from *Walking Tall* going down there. No I'm not gonna be Walking Tall, I'm gonna be Leatherface in *The Texas Chainsaw Massacre*. No, I'm gonna be Tanakura Ken in *The Yakuza*, I'm gonna be a samurai going down there. That's the most honourable, and that's who I'm going to be. He's almost deciding which heroic figure he will be by the weapon he chooses.'

Bruce Willis, whose starring roles mostly fall into the categories of fun-but-forgettable action movie or lousy action movie, casually explains how he fell into the part of Butch: 'Harvey [Keitel] has a house on the same beach as I do in California, his kids play with my kids, and he came over to the house one day to pick up his daughter. I hadn't seen him for a while and I told him, "*Reservoir Dogs* is so great" and he said, "You know, he's getting ready to do another film, come over tomorrow and I'll introduce you." I got hold of the script and I volunteered.'

'I didn't approach Bruce, though it was only because I thought his schedule wouldn't allow it. Bruce read the script and said, "Change your plans, guys, I'm dropping out of this movie and dropping into this one."'

'One of the things Bruce Willis brings to the part is that his role as the boxer Butch is similar to some of the characters he's played, except that they've never had to run the

In bad need of a good drycleaner, Jules enjoys the coffee in Jimmie's (Quentin Tarantino's) kitchen. (From Pulp Fiction*)*

gauntlet Butch does. I wanted Butch to be a complete fucking asshole. I wanted him to be basically like Ralph Meeker as Mike Hammer in Aldrich's *Kiss Me, Deadly*. I wanted him to be a bully and a jerk, except that when he's with his girlfriend Fabienne he's a sweetheart.' (In a section of the original script cut from the completed movie, Butch tells Esmaralda, his Colombian cab driver, that he feels he's done his opponent a favour by beating him to death, as the guy was probably in the doldrums of his boxing career; or, if he wasn't at his lowest ebb, it meant he was no boxer at all: 'That's what he gets for fuckin' up my sport.')

The Bonnie situation

'The third story isn't an old familiar story but an old familiar situation. The story starts with Jules and Vincent going to kill some guys. That's like the opening five minutes of every other Joel Silver movie – a bunch of guys show up and pow, pow, pow, kill somebody and then the credits start and then you see Arnold Schwarzenegger. So let's extend that whole little opening, let's hang out with them for the rest of their day and the shenanigans that follow.'

'I'm trying to make things funny which you're not used to seeing in a humorous light. I'm not necessarily doing it by trying to make fun of it – oftentimes, I'm showing it in such a realistic setting, but with the foibles of real life thrown onto this "action-adventure" situation, but like how it would really play in real life, so it's just seeming absurd.'

'In normal movies, they're too busy telling the plot to have guns go off accidentally and kill someone we don't give a damn about. But it happens, so we go down that track. And it's not just some clean little hole in the chest, it's a mess they've got to deal with, and it's a big problem. The humour to me comes from this realistic situation, and then in waltzes this complete movie creation, the Wolf – Harvey Keitel. This movie star walks in, sprinkles some movie dust, and solves the problems.'

Whereas Keitel played his tough guy role in *Dogs* to the hilt, this time he skirts deftly round the edges of self-parody. Like the professional killer he plays in *The Assassin*, the American remake of Luc Besson's thriller *Nikita*, he disposes of corpses and evidence. Unlike the former character, he doesn't remove the *corpus delicti* via acid baths, but packs everything up clean and tidy according to the rules of domestic hygiene. Suave, urbane and dinner-jacketed, he breaks off from his cocktail party (at 8.30 in the morning!) to attend to the problems caused by Vincent's accidentally blowing Marty, the last survivor of the gang of kids, all over the car's upholstery. Enthusing over the coffee provided by Jimmie (Tarantino), the Wolf is polite but curt in his practicality. ('Pretty please, with sugar on. Now clean the fuckin' car.') In this role, Keitel would be a natural for breakfast TV, charming housewives as he advises on how to get rid of those hard-to-shift bloodstains and slops of brain tissue.

'I guess if you're going to draw a parallel to the kind of comedy that's coming out in *Pulp Fiction*,' Tarantino says, 'I guess it's actually not very dissimilar to *Monty Python* – except that it's ridiculous in a more realistic way. You know in *The Holy Grail* when the

The Wolf (Harvey Keitel) settles up with Monster Joe's Truck and Tow over the bloodied Chevrolet, his morning's cleaning job completed.

guy says, "Do you want to fight about it?" and the other guy cuts off his left arm. And he still says, "Come on, it's a mere flesh wound, fight me, you coward!" So he cuts him in half and he stills says, "Yeah I'll fight you, I'll take you on."'

'There was a line with Jules and Jimmie talking that we didn't shoot. Jimmie asks what the fuck happened to the car, and Jules answers: "Jimmie, if you were inside of a car, and you were to shoot a water melon at point blank range with a nine millimetere, do you know what would happen?" "No, what?" "You'd get water melon all over!" To me, even though it's got a foot in real life, it also has a foot in *Monty Python*.'

Tarantino disputes the idea that he's made another violent movie, even more so than in *Dogs*' case. Instead he's gone for – and mostly achieved – a balance between absurd realism and the honest ethics of hardboiled fiction: 'What I'm doing is like in *The Big Sleep*, where there's a guy waiting outside the door for Bogart, and Bogart makes this other guy go out. The guy is, like, "I'm not gonna go out,' so Bogart shoots him in the leg. He's still not going, so Bogart shoots him in the hip, in the hand. Finally, the guy goes out and he gets shot, all right? It's tough stuff and that's what I'm trying to do with my violence.'

'What we're reacting to in our movies is the fact that we see a lot of action films and we like them and we respond to them, but more often than not we're disappointed by them. They stop too short. And when I say they stop too short, I don't mean in terms of gore. I couldn't care less about that – and they're pretty sufficient when it comes to that. But they stop too short in terms of balls, or even brutality, when the characters would in truth be brutal.

'Oddly enough, novels don't fall short. If Charles Willeford or Elmore Leonard or Jim Thompson decides that the truth of the character should be that he blows a guy away even when he doesn't have a gun in his hand, just because he's mad at him – if that's the truth of where he's coming from, that's the truth of where he's coming from. And I kind of get off on that, because I've been starved for it for the last ten years.'

This type of brute earnestness occurs on screen in Peckinpah's brilliant, underrated Mexican gothic, *Bring Me the Head of Alfredo Garcia*, when loser-on-the-turn Warren Oates shoots an already dead man, thinking rhetorically aloud, 'Why? Because it feels so good.' It also happens in Clint Eastwood's meditation on how a life of violence can weigh on the soul, *Unforgiven*, where as a broken old gunfighter he blows somebody away and is reprimanded with the words, 'You just shot an unarmed man!', growling back, 'Then he shoulda taken the time to arm himself!' Tarantino, naturally, appreciates these hardbitten masterpieces, and the value of a brutalism that has little to do with gore, but much to do with vicious honesty.

123

Success this time round came on both a critical and commercial level. The movie cleaned up, as expected, in Europe, and turned a good few million dollars' profit in the USA (though insider reports claim it fared less well than Miramax had hoped). In the midst of all this came the awards: the BAFTA (British Academy Award), the Golden Globe, and the Oscar, all for best original screenplay. Predating all of these, and the movie's summer (US)/autumn (Europe) "94 release, was the prize for best film – the Palme D'Or – at that Spring's Cannes Film Festival.

The award attracted a little controversy at the time. Some European (and even some American) critics felt the award should have gone to a more 'serious' contender, the latest in the *Three Colours* trilogy by Polish director Kieslowski. However the judges' panel voted nine-to-one in favour of *Pulp*, the presence of Clint Eastwood as panel chairman being taken to be significant in the outcome. A great commercial moviemaker only taken seriously himself over the last decade or so, Eastwood is on record as saying America has contributed two purely original artforms to the world, western movies and jazz music. If he's sharp enough to add *film noir* to his list, he'd clearly appreciate Tarantino's peculiarly original, brightly lit subversion of the genre.

Whatever the politics behind the award, Tarantino himself was elated: 'The Palme win, that's a big shield. When they're throwing bricks at me because my films are violent or this, that or the other, in some ways the Palme win is something that says: "You're misunderstanding me. I'm not just about that. I'm about other things too."'

'The entire time I was writing *Pulp Fiction* I was thinking, This will be my Get-It-Out-of-Your-System movie. This will be the movie where I say goodbye to the gangster genre for a while, because I don't want to be the next Don Siegel – not that I'm as good. I don't want to just be the gun guy...I've got so many [movies] I would like to make. I've got my western, my World War II bunch-of-guys-on-a-mission movie, my spaghetti western, my horror film. But since I know I won't live long enough to do all the movies I wanna do, with every movie the goal is to wipe out as many as I can. But *Pulp Fiction* is maybe even more of a kitchen sink movie than I'll probably ever make again. It really is three movies for the price of one.'

Before anyone could point out that westerns and war films have more than a little use for guns, Tarantino was equivocating back and forth over whether it was time to say goodbye to crime, *noir*, pulp, or whatever handy generic labels had been hung on him: 'I was going to do other sorts of movies, then revisit the crime genre from time to time... At the same time, fuck it, if it's what you really want to do... It's a little debate I'm having with myself because *Pulp* was designed to be the goodbye.'

'The thing about it is, what do I do?' he reflects, conscious of how he invented the post-modern pulp niche he now finds himself in. 'Do I relish it and want to go even further in that direction? Or do I say, I'm gonna show you what I can do with a bedroom comedy – same kind of dialogue, same basic movie, but without the violence? Well, I think you're kind of a fool going with either of those things. You just, you know, "To thine own self be true."'

CHAPTER 6

Natural born killers –

'Killin' you and what you represent is a statement.

I'm not exactly sure what it's sayin'...'

ndependent production team Don Murphy and Jane Hamsher (she of the part-Cherokee background incorporated into the Tarantino legend, see chapter 1) picked up on the *Natural Born Killers* script in the early days, when its author was still hopeful of receiving the backing to direct it himself. Murphy claims it was 'a complete Badlands rip-off', but, 'Quentin was a writer we knew and liked... everything he showed us was superficial, but he was talented and he had a way of putting a spin on old ideas that was original.'

Given time and rewrites, *Natural Born Killers* acquired a brutally satirical dimension, taking on board the media colonisation of crime and the murderer as celebrity. 'Now here was a cool script,' says Murphy, who was now ready to take out an option on it. The deal was a standard one for a new scriptwriter: $10,000 as an advance, plus a guaranteed $60,000 if the film was made; for every $1 million the budget rose above £10 million, the scriptwriter would receive a further $10,000.

As far as Murphy and Hamsher were concerned, they had a viable ongoing project. That is, until *Reservoir Dogs* broke, and its author tried to murder his younger baby. 'He actively campaigned against the project,' says Murphy. 'He even told Brian De Palma he'd picket the theatre if he directed it.'

Whether his concern was to wipe out any traces of the pre-*Reservoir Dogs* days, or simply to regain control and strike a more lucrative deal, Tarantino's vocal opposition nevertheless looked like sinking the project for the producers.

But, as things were looking bleakest, Murphy and Hamsher found themselves a name director. Oliver Stone was perhaps the biggest, and possibly the most incongruous Hollywood figure they could have persuaded to take the project. Known for bombastic epics, and a certain socially conscious *Sturm und Drang*, Stone agreed to start work on *Natural Born Killers* as soon as he had finished *Heaven and Earth*, the final part of the Vietnam trilogy which also comprised Platoon and *Born on the Fourth of July*.

Oliver Stone

Tutored by Martin Scorsese at film school, Oliver Stone first directed two horror movies, *Seizure* (1980) and *The Hand* (1981), the latter starring Michael Caine. Since finding fame, initially with *Platoon* and *Salvador*, his action-films-with-a-conscience, Stone has done his best to suppress his earlier work. Interestingly, however, *The Hand* found him experimenting with a mixture of colour and b&w film, switching suddenly to monochrome as the melodramatic events intensified – a technique later taken to a more audacious extreme in *Natural Born Killers*.

A 'B'-movie tribute seen through a 1960s survivor's eyes: Oliver Stone directing Natural Born Killers.

Platoon *(1986): Willem Dafoe's battered 'good sergeant' is protected from his malevolent counterpart, while new 'grunt' Charlie Sheen looks on (top left). Despite his later criticism of Oliver Stone's style, Tarantino was an admirer of* Platoon *in the mid-80s.*

Stone's initial directorial triumph came with *Platoon*, where he was able to bring raw emotion and an authentic perspective to the Vietnamese battlegrounds of his youth. (Despite this, two of the main characters, a humane sergeant and his sadistic counterpart, still play like good soldier-bad-soldier archetypes, rather than three dimensional human beings.) The film was a huge critical and commercial success, finding great favour with a young audience that included Quentin Tarantino and Roger Avary. Stone consolidated his position with *Salvador* (1987), a spirited, sometimes harrowing journey into El Salvador, a land of red hot peppers and death squads which the US used to extol as a democratic model for Central America. With an engaging performance by James Woods, as a dissipated foreign correspondent who finds himself 'getting involved' despite his better judgement, Salvador made the 24-year-old Tarantino's list of all-time favourite movies.

His biography of Jim Morrison, *The Doors* (1991), was the next landmark before *JFK* (also 1991), a sprawling three-hour story of deceit and governmental subterfuge based on the memoirs of Jim Garrison (played by Kevin Costner), an attorney who claimed, against all odds, to have uncovered part of the conspiracy that supposedly killed Kennedy. Utilising semi-verité and documentary techniques, plus the still stunning Zapruder footage (which gives it a chilly 'mondo movie' feeling), JFK is either an engrossing subversion of recent history, or an irresponsible piece of pseudo-investigation playing fast-and-loose with the facts – depending on whether you believe Oswald had any colleagues hidden behind the grassy knoll.

'I was doing *Heaven and Earth* and I did *Natural Born Killers* right after I finished,' says Stone, 'so it was sort of an explosion of guts and vomit and everything. Because *Heaven and Earth* was so much about conquering violence in yourself, about overcoming hate...maybe I wanted to have a purge of it in my life.'

'Everybody was against the movie. Everybody. My ex-wife thought it was a huge mistake, and we were divorcing, my son was doubting me, my cameraman, who'd been with me for nine movies. I lost my old producer, on other matters, but we basically split. You reach places in your life and you realise, maybe too late, that you're in a major fucking traffic accident here. So we made the movie like a traffic accident. I just kept going. We thought we'd do it cheap: rear projection, 8mm, but all that costs more than anybody knows because you have to blow it up to 35mm. So we went over budget. Then I had Tarantino complaining. It was a nightmare. All I could see was the tunnel. When I got to the prison at the end [the interview/riot scenes, filmed in a real maximum security prison], I was relieved, felt like I was home. My favourite shot is when Tommy Lee Jones looks over his shoulder and sees two thousand fucking maniacs coming at him. That's the way I felt.'

Despite all the minor traumas along the way, after the movie's US release Stone was claiming, '*Killers* has performed some happy function. I feel lighter, happier.' (As Stone's one of the few directors able to demand a good percentage deal, he was probably also feeling richer, given the movie's exceptional performance among the US youth market.) The catharsis was a violent one, however, and it has a fascinatingly twisted history.

A young man and young woman enter a Mid-Western diner. While her boyfriend orders food, the girl chooses a record on the jukebox and dances to it. Three rednecks assume she's easy meat and hassle her, trying to force themselves on her when she resists. She and her boyfriend pull guns, slaughtering nearly everyone in the diner. The waitress begs to be spared, but the girl chooses a redneck to be the only survivor, so that he can tell the media the crimes were committed by Mickey and Mallory. 'How sexy am I now?' screams Mallory to the redneck corpses littering the floor.

Mallory's family background is related in the form of a TV situation comedy called I Love Mallory. *Dad is a drunken, incestuous old slob, while Mom is a browbeaten moral coward who puts up with all her husband's excesses (including rape of her daughter) because she knows no better. Her little brother is a passive witness who says little, wearing face make-up based on that of the heavy metal band Kiss. Audience approval greets the entrance of Mallory's boyfriend Mickey, the meat delivery boy, much like the standard cheers for Fonzie in* Happy Days. *Very soon, however, Mickey is arrested by the police for an earlier offence.*

Mickey escapes from his rural prison on a horse. The scene takes place in vintage B-western style, on faded black and white footage. He returns to Mallory's home, where the style reverts to that of a sitcom. Mickey and Mallory kill her parents – the old man is beaten, slashed and drowned in a fish tank, her mother incinerated in her bed. Studio audience cheers greet the 'setting free' of her little brother.

On a high bridge over a deep gorge, Mickey and Mallory clasp cut hands in a blood bond: an ad hoc marriage ceremony on the road. As a carload of jeering assholes careers by, Mickey pledges: 'No killing anybody on our wedding day.' By this point in the narrative (the opening diner massacre occurring chronologically later), the audience has only seen Mickey shoot a prison guard and kill Mallory's parents, but he's obviously resolved on a life of random murder.

A crime-exploitation TV show, American Maniacs, *becomes a vehicle of the narrative, encapsulating 'the story of Mickey and Mallory' so far. Hosted by oily Australian presenter Wayne Gale, it's a kind of* Lifestyles of the Sick and Infamous, *the opening credits announcing its intentions with shots of those all-American celebrities, Charlies Manson and Whitman ('University of Texas massacre' sniper), Richard Ramirez ('the Night Stalker') and Richard Speck (murderer of eight nurses in one frenzied night).*

On the road, Mickey suggests several passing women to capture and kill. Mallory is annoyed by his chauvinism and sets off to make a kill herself. She enters a garage workshop where she seduces a mechanic on the bonnet of a car, the coupling turning into a violent struggle before she shoots him dead, ostensibly for giving 'the worst head I ever had'.

Returning to Mickey, the couple run out of gas in the middle of the desert. An old American Indian shaman takes them into his hut. He seems able to see into their souls, and has some sympathy for them. He gives them a drink which seems to contain peyote, as Mickey hallucinates during the night, reliving his own childhood abuse, and kills the old man in his terror. The killing meets Mallory's deep disapproval. The shaman's revenge soon comes down on the couple, in the form of a plague of rattlesnakes. Their desperate, delirious search for snake antidote – intercut with cartoon footage showing the pair as muscular 'manga'-style superheroes – leads to the murder of a Hawaiian drug store owner. M & M are arrested during the police response, which is led by Detective Jack Scagnetti, who has been obsessively on their trail and has developed a perverse infatuation with Mallory.

One year later, Scagnetti is called in by the warden of the prison where both Mickey and Mallory are held separately in solitary confinement. Conspiratorial agreement is reached that Scagnetti will kill them both, eliminating the subversive influence the warden believes their presence is having over the prison. The detective is a celebrity lawman, author of the book Scagnetti on Scagnetti, *and is intolerant of any attempt to psychoanalyse or empathise with murderers. This attitude originates in a flashback scene where the boy*

Scagnetti witnesses his mother being blown away by Charles Whitman, at the University of Texas massacre.

On Superbowl Sunday, Wayne Gale is granted the in-depth interview with Mickey Knox he has been trying for. He conducts it in an uppity, sanctimonious manner recalling the time Geraldo Rivera went fishing for ratings with Charles Manson from the high moral ground. Mickey's self-contented comment that he's just a 'natural born killer' sparks a riot among the maximum security prisoners who are watching him on TV, fully aware of his presence among them for the first time. While the guards are distracted, Mickey grabs a shotgun and kills several of them, leading a procession of hostages through the prison to Mallory's cell. He finds Scagnetti trying to rape her, and blows him away. The couple fight their way out via the front gate, accompanied by Gale, who is shedding mortally wounded cameramen along the way. The infernal riot converts Gale into a born-again nihilist, shrieking, 'I feel alive for the first time ever!'

On the outside, Mickey decides that Gale's attitude is incompatibly opposed to theirs,

Mallory Knox (Juliette Lewis) shows her deadly proficiency with a gun, to husband Mickey's (Woody Harrelson) cool admiration, in Natural Born Killers *(1994).*

no matter how he feels. His amorally liberated mind is still fixed on ratings, whereas – despite the ludicrous number of people they've killed inside jail in the year since they've been incarcerated – they just want a new life together. Once his imploring to have faith in the TV medium is exhausted, the quaking Gale stands in cruciform, waiting to die in a clearing in the woods. 'Killin' you is a statement,' consoles his executioner, 'though I'm not exactly sure what its sayin'.' Gale is shot dead while his own camera films the event.

The ending is almost sentimental: Mickey and Mallory renounce murder in favour of staying free and making a baby – not because they've undergone any kind of moral reformation, but because, with all that killing, they've got it out of their systems at last. As Mickey tried to explain to Gale, there was never any philosophy behind their crimes, they were never interested in murder. Violence and hate was their heritage, bequeathed to them by the circumstances of their birth. Now that they've performed all the evil deeds any two people could possibly dream of, murder is just something that goes on outside of them – as evidenced by apocalyptic news clips which close the movie, intercut with a flash-forward showing M & M living quietly and happily together in a trailer home.

Whatever Tarantino's reaction to the completed *Natural Born Killers*, of his two orphaned road movies, *Killers* stands in the same relation to *Apocalypse Now* as *Romance* does to *Taxi Driver*. While Tony Scott's film – as exciting a ride as it is – does not have a tenth of the intensity of Paul Schrader and Martin Scorsese's masterpiece, Stone's unfaithful adaptation takes its similar but divergent core material into the realms of acid psychosis.

Killers was taken seriously in many critical quarters – albeit not universally – as is shown by some of the reviews that greeted its summer 1994 US release: 'A satirical indictment of our societal fascination with violence and killers,' said *The New York Times*. Most pertinently, *Variety* claimed it was, 'Possibly the most hallucinatory and anarchic picture made at a major Hollywood studio in at least twenty years... a psychedelic documentary about the American cult of sex, violence and celebrity.'

If rewound to the late 70s, Tarantino's retentive cinematic memory would recall how *Apocalypse Now* was berated by many who revered *Taxi Driver*, for what they considered its acid-trip trivialisation of the horrors of war. *Taxi Driver*, on the other hand, was considered the more 'serious' film for depicting its intensifying madness as an internal process, articulated in the voice-over by De Niro, and in its downplaying of the 'deranged Viet vet' elements. (Vietnam is never mentioned, only alluded to when Travis, the De Niro character explains that he spent three years in the marines before coming to Manhattan, and when at the climax he 'gets into character' with cropped hair and camouflage fatigues.)

These days, it's common for many people to rate both *Taxi Driver* and *Apocalypse Now* among their favourite films, as Tarantino does. Back then, the externalised psychic chaos of Coppola's movie was seen as too excessive to have much cinema-snob appeal. Compared to *Natural Born Killers*, however, it's a pallid exercise in restraint.

From the opening diner massacre – with its askew angles, manic editing, and rapid transitions from b & w to full enhanced colour – to the final apocalyptic montage, *Killers* was deliberately designed to avoid Hollywood conventions. During the massacre itself, Tarantino's original script is adhered to fairly faithfully; the camera's point of view follows the trajectory of a bullet heading towards a short-order cook, as written – but Stone takes it one step further, having the lead projectile hang frozen momentarily in the air, as if in a comic book, before reaching its target.

It's this process of exaggerating the source material to the nth degree, of using the original script as the starting point for a race through a kind of TV Hell, that may have prompted the newly arrived wunderkind to remove his name from the screenwriting credits. Despite the sequences that stick closely to his own conception, the movie's development is brutally linear, moving from point A to point Z on a flight-path through as much visual information as the overloaded viewer can stand. The stark rawness of Tarantino's nihilist B-movie concept consequently gets lost, Stone's approach being alien enough for Tarantino to opt for story credit only. This is, in essence, accurate – Tarantino's story survives in a basic form, but with all perspectives and emphases switched around. The mockery of self-righteous tabloid TV is still a mainstay of the movie: 'You're not even an ape,' Mickey tells slimy American Maniacs anchorman Wayne Gale (Robert Downey Jnr), 'you're a media person.' ('From where you're standing you're a man. From where I'm standing you're an ape,' opines Tarantino's Mickey without malice, claiming to have evolved from the type of half-blind Everyman he perceives Gale to be. In the filmed version, the director changes the line to make his obvious satirical intentions re the media even clearer.) Stone's idea of satire is as upfront and frenetic as every other aspect of the movie, with Downey playing Gale as a cartoonishly reptilian piece of bullet fodder no-one can ultimately sympathise with. However, while Tarantino's original script centres around the theme of serial murder as a media event, with much of the narrative working as a pastiche of the *Geraldo/ Current Affair/ America's Most Wanted* format, Stone decided to paint on a wider canvas. First of all, the kissin' and killin' couple had to become more central to the development of the (minimal) plot, rather than just the subject of what's happening around them. 'I wanted to go more into Mickey and Mallory,' he explains, 'more into the socio-political surround; the concept of violence and aggression in everything.'

One of the subtle but integral changes of emphasis and intent, between Tarantino's original and Stone's adaptation, comes in the following line of dialogue: 'Was an instant of purity worth a lifetime lie? Yeah, it was,' says Tarantino's Mickey, reflecting on the murder spree that took him from being a nobody in a burger joint to the most infamous mass murderer in the USA. Stone's Mickey, on the other hand, tells Wayne Gale: 'An instant of my purity is worth a lifetime of your lies.' It's a subtle switch from the personal to the social – Mickey no.1 telling how he doesn't regret leaving his nowhere existence behind, no matter how extreme the mode of escape, Mickey no.2 sneering at the phoniness of the media and the society which made him what he is. It's also indicative of the conflicting intent of the scriptwriter who wanted to tell the story of two

Don't look back: Mickey and Mallory about to flee a murder scene and hit the road to hell.

typical B-movie lowlifes, and the director who wanted to make a movie reflecting what situationist theoreticians once called 'the society of the spectacle'.

That said, Stone has to be credited for making a frenetic, almost chaotic kaleidoscope of violent media imagery that no mere careerist would chance. It's also true that the director – who seems to have been reading his Nietzsche – philosophises with a hammer; there's not a single image among all the quickfire edits that has any kind of slow-burn subtlety, everything smacks the viewer directly in the face. Stone's personal comment on the media's exploitation of violence (rather than Tarantino's, which is a more specific swipe at the US TV programmes which pretend to a moral loftiness while milking serial killers for all their worth) is honest – or perhaps confused – enough to include the movies: bloody scenes from *The Wild Bunch*, *Midnight Express* and De Palma's *Scarface* grow from the TV screen till they seem to cover the wall of Mickey and Mallory's motel room. ('What is it with all these stupid movies?' bemoans Mickey, no fan of violence in the media. 'Ain't anyone interested in kissing anymore?') If we're to take Mr Stone literally – and it's hard to know when to and when not to, as the irony that's surely present is most often buried beneath visual excess – then this seems to be a confession of his own complicity: *Midnight Express* and *Scarface* were both early Stone script assignments (he received an Academy Award nomination for the former), and contained within *Killers'* psychotic tableaux are the bloodiest moments from each histrionic epic – the biting and spitting-out of a prison guard's tongue from *Midnight Express*, and the chainsaw murder of a hood in *Scarface*. 'Demon...too much TV' is one of the written messages filtered across Mallory's body – most of the movie's visuals commenting on the narrative itself, rather than simply appearing in context. It seems like a visual joke at the expense of Stone's own heavy-handed symbolism, though it's by no means clear. (The other movie clip, beside the violent epics above, is from James Whale's 1931 *Frankenstein*. The analogy between Karloff's scientifically misbegotten Monster and M & M Knox is pretty obvious – society/TV/trash culture made me, now they want to destroy me when I run amok.)

Other images are appropriated from newsreel footage, rather than the literalised Tarantinoism of movie quotation: Hitler and Stalin make back-projected appearances, the historic scale of their crimes out of proportion to the parochial mass murder taking place in the movie. (Which is perhaps the point Stone is making – see his comments at the end of the chapter.)

The original images which flash almost subliminally on and off screen are no subtler. Hellfire, blood, demons (the three-eyed and fanged Hieronymous Bosch variety) all appear in animated form, adding a certain infernal ambience to Mickey and Mallory's activities, even at their calmest. The viewer either comes to terms with these bad-trip-cum-*Bedknobs and Broomsticks* effects, or else just develops cinematic indigestion. As far as the execution may be from Tarantino's original concept, it makes an exhilarating experience for that part of the movie audience reared on bizarre spectacle. All the berserk imagery, the back-projected visuals, are assimilated into a format that cuts quickly, alarmingly, sometimes jarringly, between colour and b & w, celluloid and video,

35mm and Super-8. As Stone has admitted, the movie is based on a TV channel-surfing mentality, with as much information as the viewer can swallow, or in this case, the same basic information shown via different visual media, before becoming overloaded. One detail that *Natural Born Killers* has in common with Tarantino's own *Pulp Fiction* which, by virtue of its almost simultaneous completion date, became an official rival to *Killers* at the box office – following it by a couple of months in the US, preceding it by the same period in Britain – is that both were edited on Lightworks. This new computer-based system enables a film to be digitally edited at high-speed in many different versions, facilities which Stone and his editors made full use of.

'We always planned mixed media,' explains Stone, 'because of the video component in the film, the TV crew in the prison. But then as we worked on it we decided to go into dream state. We decided on rear projection as a way to show what they were feeling, or…a concept of collective unconscious for the century.'

While Oliver Stone aspires to be the Carl Jung of the high-tech age, his detractors accuse *Killers* of MTV sensibilities – which is, of course part of the culture he's trying to satirise. However, whereas MTV's videos long ago appropriated the eccentric angles and frenetic cutting of experimental filmmaking, Stone has returned the now-clichéd form to the cinema screen, where its pervasive effect is harder to ignore, its impact much more direct. *Killers'* overall effect is one of cinematic phantasmagoria, which, despite its brutally in-your-face subject matter, only rarely comes close to (or even tries to attain) any kind of realism.

'It reflects the junkyard culture of the time,' says Stone. 'It has a TV sensibility where everything is visually changing, channel-surfing, coming at you. But stylistically, we also wanted to enter into the head of two killers, make it subjective, hallucinatory. They've watched a lot of TV. They're desensitised to it. She lives in a sitcom. So the idea was to stay unpredictable.'

Given Tarantino's liking for Italian exploitation movies and the vividness of *Apocalypse Now*, his subsequent squabbles with Stone may be less to do with the rollercoaster-ride-through-hell approach than with Stone's and co-writer Richard Rutowski's alterations and additions to the script.

Stone's first major addition – his own conception, honed into shape with his co-writer – is the *I Love Mallory* sitcom sequence. Totally absent from the original script, the scene is one of the most effective in the movie: as her rapist-slob old man and weakling mother make her life a misery – the only reason Mallory has a little brother is because the old man was so drunk one night he screwed the old lady, believing he was in Mallory's room – the studio audience roar with laughter at each detail of abuse. To the viewer, this is one of the blackest pieces of screen comedy seen in the last decade. (It seems to echo a soap-opera pastiche in one of Richard Kern's *Death Trip* films, which ends with the teenage heroine shooting all of her family. There's also a passing resemblance to the tacky trash-culture humour of John Waters – or even George Kuchar, whose short films influenced both Waters and Kern.) To Stone, it's also a means of giving a context to Mallory's rage and hatred, an element missing from the original script.

'There's so much pain in her, she distances herself,' says Stone, 'filters it as a memory so that it just becomes part of the TV channel-surf trip. Nonetheless, it certainly affected her. The movie is subjective, always in their mind. I'm being ironic, yes, but also imagining how she might deal with that.'

The other scene with no roots at all in the Tarantino script was the sequence of events at the Indian's shack. The encounter with the shaman – who fatalistically moans, 'I dreamed 20 years ago the demons would come' – is straight out of the trippier moments of Stone's *The Doors* which for the most part took Jim Morrison's claims of white shamanism seriously. In fact it's so incongruous that it seems to belong to another film entirely.

It's little credited that Stone actually noted Tarantino's own original suggestions for the shooting format – video for segments that double as TV reportage, grainy super-8mm with bad sound for the courtroom scenes – and took them to their wildest extreme. The result is far less akin to Tarantino (who, after all, is mainly influenced by mainstream movie-makers) than it is to some of the young underground filmmakers from the 'Cinema of Transgression', who Stone may not have even heard of before he made *Killers*.

If any part of the movie epitomises how it reaches way beyond its B-movie-influenced source material, it's the ending and closing credits. Leonard Cohen's song, 'The Future' – a smooth jeremiad from adult-orientated rock's very own Old Testament prophet – plays over the closing images, and the credit sequence which sees the escaped young homicidal honeys, Mickey and Mallory, driving off to a happy new life together. 'Things are gonna slide, slide in all directions, nothing you can cling to or measure any more... I have seen The Future, it is Murder,' growls the pessimistic poet, hammering home that everything you've just seen is about as far from a Tarantino celebration of trash culture as you can get. In the same way the song, with its plea, 'Give me back the Berlin Wall, give me Stalin and Saint Paul, give me Christ and give me Hiroshima', rather than the uncertainty and random violence of 'The Future', is light years removed from any vintage bubblegum classic on the soundtrack of *Reservoir Dogs* or *Pulp Fiction*. This ain't just plain old movie magic – as if anyone hadn't realised that by now – this is a Statement.

The closing sequence is intercut with various bits of contemporary news footage: the siege at Waco, Texas, as the sanctuary of David Koresh and his followers is blown to hell in an FBI raid; the trial of Lorena Bobbitt, feminist-icon severer of her macho husband's penis; the Menedez brothers, poor little rich boys who pleaded sex abuse by Daddy as mitigation in their trial for blasting their millionaire parents to death at close range; and the committal proceedings against O. J. Simpson, just opening as the film finished production.

'The media *per se* is just a robot, it's capitalism run rampant,' opines Stone. 'What they do, they create non-events. Two ice skaters have a fight, and that becomes the basis for the winter Olympics getting the biggest ratings ever. Lorena Bobbitt – that would

Mickey in front of the cartoon imagery that comes phantasmagorically to life.

have been in the *National Enquirer* when I was growing up. It goes beyond crime, it goes to distort public policy.'

If such a wide selection of contemporary American cases bears a single interpretation, it's something like this: justice, as we understood it, was only a fragile concept, and its hold is now gone; we can no longer look to the law for protection, it's simply a part of the circus of absurdities; all we can seek to do is to meet the madness around us on its own terms. Or something like that.

Oliver Stone clearly relished his adopted role as social soothsayer and contentious commentator: 'When we set out to make *Natural Born Killers* in late 1992, it was surreal. By the time it was finished in 1994, it had become real...In my movie, Mickey says to the TV type who's hounding him and Mallory that you must acknowledge the shadow in yourself. Society itself casts a violent shadow and we can't separate ourselves from it just by throwing all our violent characters into jail. That's no solution. The aggression problem will be solved by recognition that it exists.'

So *Natural Born Killers*, to its director, is nothing less than diagnosis of a social pandemic. In a sense, he's spot on, but Stone's attitudes fly beyond his astute appropriation of modern 'transgressive' attitudes, into an uncritical acceptance of one of its icons, one Charles M. Manson: 'In making the movie we were very influenced by the interview [Manson] did in his jail cell with Geraldo, the chat-show host, in the 1980s. Manson runs intellectual circles round Geraldo – yet Geraldo considers himself superior to Manson the whole time... In my view, Manson was prosecuted in an atmosphere of social hysteria. It was a bit of a witch trial.'

As might be anticipated, all this cultural baggage is anathema to Tarantino's way of thinking, and is far removed from his basic story of a guy, his girl, their guns, and the TV presenter who feeds off of them. No enthusing about movies and pop culture for Oliver Stone (though the imagery of *Killers* is saturated with them, it's far from celebratory) – his approach is, let's talk social apocalypse.

In a short space of time, the initial gap between Tarantino and Stone grew into resentment, festered into a grudge, then turned into a slanging match. 'You don't have to worry about seeing me in *Natural Born Killers*: you'll only see Oliver Stone,' complained Tarantino, disowning those elements of his script which still remained. 'His voice is so loud that people who like it give him the credit. People who don't like it are nicer to me. It's like, "Who knows what Tarantino meant?"'

'He and I are pretty much at odds as far as our sensibilities and styles are concerned. I don't like to show things. I like things unexplained. He's obviously not into that. I would imagine that if Oliver Stone showed his movie to a thousand people and a thousand people didn't exactly get the point that he was trying to make, he would think he failed. To me the best thing about him is his energy. But his biggest problem is that his obviousness cancels out his energy and his energy pumps up his obviousness. He's Stanley Kramer with style.'

'When I met him, I said, "You're a good film maker. Why don't you do smaller – why don't you do a movie?" I was saying to him more or less, "Why don't you do

The greasy face of law and order: Detective Scagnetti (Tom Sizemore) and the Warden (Tommy Lee Jones) are shown to be at least as corrupt in their way as Mickey and Mallory.

something like *Reservoir Dogs?*" And he goes, "Well, that's what I'm doing with *Natural Born Killers.*" And I go, "No, you're not. It's *Oliver Stone Takes on Serial Killers and Violence in America.* It's just as big, if not bigger, than anything you've ever done." And he said, "*Reservoir Dogs* is very good, but it's a movie. I make films and you make movies. Martin Scorsese, he makes movies. John Woo, he makes movies. But after you've been working for 15 years, you may look back and say, 'Hey, all I've done is make a bunch of movies,' and you might want to try and make a film someday." He meant it in a kind of condescending way, but I was thinking about it later and realised he's right. I don't want to make films. I like movies. But I have no doubt that – good, bad or indifferent – *Natural Born Killers* will be interesting. I have a *Platoon* game. I really would love to play it with Oliver. But him and me are too much on the outs.'

'You're in your 20s. [Tarantino was actually hitting 30 by this time.] You're making movies about movies,' accused Stone at a meeting called by the producers supposedly to resolve the two parties' differences. 'I'm making movies about the life I've lived to my 40s. I've seen more violence than you've ever seen in your life. I've been in Vietnam. I've been shot. If you want to talk about violence, let's get real.'

Stone still insisted, with some credibility, that the completed *Killers* was a lot closer to the kind of movies Tarantino was influenced by than the disgruntled writer would admit: 'In a way, in my secret mind, this is a kind of B-film. Because it's B-film subject matter. The way Tarantino wrote it, it was a Roger Corman homage. This was used material. All that darkness you give into, you can be bleak, you can make everybody lousy and mean, you don't have to have nobility. That's what B-films gave people, that freedom just to be down and dirty.'

After the movie's production, he would add: 'I hope he likes *Natural Born Killers.* But I'm not holding my breath on it... And yeah, I'd be glad to play the game with him.'

(Woody Harrelson, who stars as Mickey, also put his ten cents worth into the controversy: 'I didn't see the redeeming qualities in the first draft of the script. It was only after Richard Rutowski and Oliver took a pass at it that you started to see it was funny.')

It's not clear whether Tarantino's sourness about the film sprang entirely from the way he predicted Stone would use the material, or whether his loss of control played a part. Producers Don Murphy and Jane Hamsher claim that Tarantino's new representative, from the William Morris Agency, called up Stone and asked him to wait until the time limit had expired on their option, so that a new deal could be negotiated to her client's advantage. When pressed, Stone would neither confirm nor deny their story. In a switch on standard Hollywood protocol, the small fry were not squeezed out, and *Natural Born Killers* remained basically an independent production.

Under the terms of his original contract however, Tarantino became eligible for a payment of $350,000 at the completion of production. As he confessed to Roger Avary, on receiving his cheque, 'My tears of sorrow turned to tears of joy. And I laughed...'

But the bile didn't stop flowing. Tarantino put it around that he had been ripped off on the deal, had suffered nothing less than 'skullduggerous theft', and his script had been ruined. His reservations regarding Oliver Stone as a director turned to outright disdain. Chided by Stone for condemning the movie sight unseen, he made a big point of going with the movie's co-star, Juliette Lewis, to a theatre showing *Natural Born Killers*, then leaving after the first 20 minutes of the film. 'I'll catch it sometime when I'm in a hotel that has cable,' was his dismissive comment.

At the same time, Tarantino wanted his original script for *Natural Born Killers* to form the latest in a series of his illustrated movie screenplays, published by Grove Atlantic in the USA and Faber & Faber in Britain. (Sales of *Pulp Fiction* are phenomenal: 165,000 copies in the UK in a year.) The only hitch was he did not have the publishing rights, having sold the script of *Natural Born Killers* outright. 'We were more than willing to let it be published', claims Don Murphy. 'The only terms we asked for were that Quentin had to stop badmouthing a movie he's never seen. He didn't shut up, and we never gave him the rights.' (Eventually, Tarantino won out and the script was published in book form in late 1995.)

Ironically, *Killers* has taken more money in the USA than any other film Tarantino has been associated with and the Mickey & Mallory look came into vogue among teenagers – basically a Californian re-run of the 70s New York Punk ripped jeans and skimpy T-shirt fetish.

Its popularity worried the American moral Right, who even before its release – in fact, from the time of pre-release publicity – attacked *Killers* and Warner Brothers for encouraging violence (the anti-Warner Bros campaign was already well underway, dating back to their release of Ice-T's *Cop Killer* album). By the time they actually found a real-life case they could label a copycat, some kind of wish-fulfillment prophecy seemed to be in effect.

Eleven murders were also supposedly 'connected' with the film – including several in France, where a boy-girl murder partnership briefly ran amok. This was used as ammunition by the British tabloids, delaying its release for several months, despite several cuts additional to the already censored US release print. In the end, even James Ferman, head of the highly sensitive British Board of Film Classification, came out against the Ban-It Brigade, stating there was no proven connection at all between the film and any of the crimes.

In essence, this was right. Some local sheriff opining 'they wuz actin' just like Mickey an' Mallory in that movie,' or 'the murders are straight out of *Natural Born Killers*' (not surprising, when M & M kill with guns, knives and by strangulation – how many methods are there left?) hardly exonerates the defendants and replaces them in the dock with Oliver Stone.

Still, there may be a link between young murderers and the film's two (anti-)heroes, although not one of direct causality. In Texas, a 13-year-old girl was decapitated by a 14-year-old boy, supposedly claiming he 'wanted to be famous like the natural born killers'. With such obvious pathological tendencies he's precisely the kind of adolescent *Natural Born Killers* takes its cue from: brooding, alienated, resentful, insecure to the

Nightmare of depravity: would Natural Born Killers *have been more acceptable to the USA's moral Right if Mickey had still been in chains at the end of the film – or if it had not been produced by Warner Bros., distributors of the infamous Cop Killer rap song?*

point of doubting his own existence, until he has committed some bloody, irrevocable act to convince himself he stands for something in this world.

Natural Born Killers and *True Romance* were the two movies fingered by Republican Senator of Kansas and presidential hopeful Bob Dole as totally morally reprehensible 'nightmares of depravity' – not so much a symptom of American social decay as its primary cause. Tarantino himself has stated that he believes the book which articulates the violence-begins-at-the-movies creed, Michael Medved's *Hollywood Versus America*, will be one of those moral tracts which become a quaint cultural artefact, much like Dr Frederic Wertham's *Seduction of the Innocent*, which fingered comic books as the root cause of juvenile delinquency in the 50s.

'It's like [affects mock southern drawl]: that nigger music is turning the white man into an animal. It can turn a woman into a slut, virgins into whores. Every ten years, there's a book which comes along and says there's violence in the streets, people are starving, anarchy brewing – blame the playmakers. It's their fault.'

Medved's attack on *Natural Born Killers* is that of an apparently sincere, concerned, conservative family man, whose vocabulary does not include the word 'satire': 'The problem is not the subject of serial killers but the way [Stone] has made them get away with what they do. He makes Mickey and Mallory cool and sexy. There is no blame. That is the response of the young audience who come out of the cinema. That is an immoral and irresponsible message.'

Oliver Stone has naturally revelled in the controversy, the cut-and-thrust of a totally confused debate: 'The world is violent and we're swamped in it this century. So I mirror that – I'm a distorting mirror, like in the circus. I'm making the point that the killers have been so idealised and glorified by the media that the media become worse than the killers.'

Self-professed 'democratic liberal' Medved may justifiably feel that he's close to having the last laugh, with the congressional leader of a newly confident Republican Party naming all Hollywood's worst offences against society as those originating in the imagination of its current Boy Wonder. Interestingly, as former *Modern Review* editor Toby Young has noted, no such condemnation stretched to the sporadically violent and drug-fixated *Pulp Fiction*, which co-stars high-profile Republican supporter Bruce Willis.

'It is a confused and unresolved message,' says Medved of *Killers*. 'The film is an intellectual mess. It is a psychotic indulgence which glorifies violence like nothing else in recent film history.'

As if to give the finger to a moralist like Medved, Stone has indulged in a bout of mutual endorsement with the sub-generation to whom *Natural Born Killers* makes perfect sense. Stepping down a couple of decades from his own middle age, he talks of identifying with the more subterranean school of post-grunge rockers (like Trent Reznor of Nine Inch Nails, and Eddie Vedder of Pearl Jam), and echoes some of the sentiments of the loosely knit wave of 'aesthetic nihilists', most of whom are based around the West Coast: 'My little boy has seen *Natural Born Killers* five times. He has the soundtrack too. He loves the soundtrack. By the way, I didn't force the kid to see it. You have to allow for the fact that in America today there's already a well-rooted alternative culture among the young. These kids are talking different technologies. They're calling into question all the values that have gone before... they're talking of violence and murder in less absolute terms... as things that are relative. As our century ends, it's been estimated that some hundred million violent deaths have occurred. So 52 people slain by Mickey and Mallory in *Natural Born Killers* doesn't seem such a big deal. I think the kids have the measure of that irony.' (Perhaps he would have served himself better by saying, '52 people slain by Mickey and Mallory in a movie doesn't seem such a big deal.')

The last comment belongs to Oliver Stone, as he elaborates on his movie's seemingly infinite message, but at last brings it firmly down to earth – to 1990s USA: 'Violent crime in the States is actually statistically flat per capita. It's the perception of it which has accelerated to enormous proportions, only because the media can make money selling it. And it's worked, to the degree that polls show that violent crime is the number one concern of the voter – so you get more of a law-and-order society promised. Basically, more fascism is what you get: more cops, more prisons, more oppression. Fear is the future.'

CHAPTER 7

Hollywood after Quentin

When *Reservoir Dogs* first appeared in 1992, it was on the crest of a worldwide wave of visceral thrillers that included Ferrara's *Bad Lieutenant* and the Belgian movie, *Man Bites Dog*: 'the New Brutalism', as critics were fond of labelling it at the time.

By the time of *Pulp Fiction*'s release in 1994, Tarantino was the only filmmaker among his 'new brutalist' contemporaries to have developed a distinctive, maverick style of commercial cinema. (Apart from Ferrara, who continues in his own willfully perverse way, with wildly different, but always interesting, results.) Since the release of his second feature, and the attendant controversy that surrounded *Natural Born Killers*, Tarantino has consolidated the reputation acquired by his debut feature to the point where he's become a movie-making yardstick. At the time of *Pulp*'s release, the film critic John Powers referred to the 'Quentin-ization of Hollywood'. Apart from the tendency of both the press and the movie-going public to hang onto his every effusive word, it nows seems as if the consecutive advents of *Dogs* and were a kind of Year Zero for aspiring young commercial filmmakers. At this point in the 1990s, any new director who dares to tackle an urban crime theme, or to use violence in a stylish, witty manner, finds themselves either acclaimed as making or accused of having tried to make the new *Reservoir Dogs* or *Pulp Fiction*.

Tarantino has reflected on the phenomenal growth of his cult status over the last two years: 'I think my biggest appeal amongst young fans is they look at me as a fan boy who made it.' At his January 1995 National Film Theatre appearance, he extended on this by claiming: 'If you love movies enough, you can make them. You don't have to know a camera lens from a bag of sand.'

This explanation is fine as far as it goes, and it certainly relates to the element of fandom that sees Tarantino's success as their own lifestyle venerated. But it overlooks the vast majority of his audience who are not nascent moviemakers, who don't even have vague dreams about making a film one day. To them, 'Tarantino' is a genre: to many, the name conjures all the obvious factors, the blood, the guns, the casual use of obscenity in the dialogue, all of which characteristics are shared with other action thrillers. To his more attentive fans, the movies are equal parts subversion of standard genre expectations, black comedy and trash culture celebration, with implicit movie references woven into the fabric of the script.

The movie scripts of *Dogs* and *Pulp* have become bestsellers in their own right, and their soundtrack albums are regular fixtures on many bar jukeboxes. Compiled carefully by Tarantino himself, they feature key dialogue extracts strategically placed alongside the pop-funk, kitsch country and surf rock cuts, with calorie-laden titles like 'Let's Get a Taco' and 'Royale With Cheese'. It's the first time since the vivid audio double album of Coppola's *Apocalypse Now* that a painstaking effort has been made to reproduce part of a movie's effect on disc, rather than just raking in a few extra bucks by making the music available to fanatical collectors. (Bruce Willis admitted to Tarantino that, before he got the part of Butch in *Pulp*, he would spend afternoons at home with his brothers 'riffing on scenes from *Dogs*'.)

Although only connected at several removes, the similarly definitive *Killers* soundtrack, *Music from and Inspired by Natural Born Killers*, compiled by Trent Reznor of Nine Inch Nails, could only benefit from the fan market that currently eats up all things Tarantino. Produced on a similar brief to Tarantino's own albums – though it omits a few soundtrack contributions and replaces them with equally powerful cuts recorded for the project – the most notable dialogue snippets tend to come from Juliette Lewis, with her 'I see Angels' speech accompanied by the Cowboy Junkies' cover of 'Sweet Jane', and her venomous remark to the garage hand she's in the process of killing: 'That's the worst fucking head I ever got in my life.'

Quizzed on his immediate plans after *Pulp Fiction*, Tarantino answered non-committally: 'I'm basically lazy, and to get me to stop enjoying life it's gotta be something that I really wanna do. I'm gonna take almost a year off. I remember when I was younger I wanted to be like Fassbinder, 42 films in ten years. Now that I've made a couple I don't want it.' Thus began the busiest hiatus in the history of the entertainment industry. Apparently, the concept of a 'year off' for Tarantino meant little or no time actually directing a cast and crew – though even here, his manic productivity occasionally won out over the desire to take it easy and enjoy.

First of the 'relaxation' projects was his second bit-part in a non-Tarantino film. (The first was *Sleep With Me* – see chapter 4.) *Somebody To Love* was directed in the latter half of 1994 by Alexandre Rockwell, whose comedy-drama *In The Soup* previewed alongside *Reservoir Dogs* at the 1992 Sundance Film Festival. (*In The Soup* also starred Steve Buscemi, probably the only actor rehearsing two projects simultaneously at Sundance in 1991.)

Somebody To Love picked up one or two reservedly admiring reviews, but overall the response was no more than lukewarm. Ostensibly occupying an East LA lowlife milieu that Tarantino himself might have felt comfortable with, this dark comedy about love and the desperation to make a buck has a concept which reads more intensely than it plays on screen. It stars the ubiquitous Harvey Keitel as Harry, a small-time actor forever on the verge of leaving his wife for his young Hispanic lover, Mercedes (Rosie Perez). She in turn is pursued by a younger man, Ernesto (Michael DeLorenzo), who

Alexandre Rockwell's In The Soup *(1992). Rockwell's film appeared in the same Sundance Festival as* Reservoir Dogs, *and Rockwell became a close friend of Tarantino's.*

ultimately commits a contract killing to raise the $10,000 she claims to need, but which is actually for Harry so that he can leave his wife and return to New York. The storyline has all the ingredients of great *noir*, but is played in a dreamy, disengaged manner that recalls the Americana-at-a-remove of European directors like Wim Wenders, or those directors who re-absorbed their native culture via a filter of European sensibilities, like Jim Jarmusch.

Most symptomatic of the movie's approach is a flashback sequence where Harry tells about his failed attempt to play a gorilla on TV. The sequence is funny, but seems disconnected from the rest of the movie, as do the characters from each other. Clearly, Tarantino's ability in *Pulp Fiction* to draw a whole host of disparate elements into an electrifying whole can't be attained just by trying a similar schtick.

That said, some critics were unnecessarily harsh on *Somebody To Love*, overlooking its moody photography and oddball atmosphere. Rockwell was attacked for supposedly playing the 'famous friends' card, having not only legitimately featured *Dogs* stars Keitel and Buscemi in lead/supporting roles, but also utilised small cameos from Anthony Quinn, Tarantino as the bartender at the club where Mercedes works, Eddie Bunker, and Sam Fuller in the role of 'Old Man on Highway'.

If *Somebody To Love*'s appropriation of Euro-art film style was considered a mild offence in some quarters, the movie which features Tarantino's next, more substantial role (if only in the sense of occupying more screentime) was a major felony. *Destiny Turns on the Radio*, directed by Jack Baran, was in production at virtually the same time as Rockwell's film. Occupying similar trash-Americana-through-art-house-screen territory, it's basically a road movie with pretensions.

The plot tells of a love triangle between two small-time thieves and an adaptable girlfriend. In the pivotal incident of the story the hoods are ripped off, not by a third hood – an obvious device which might have placed us in familiar but effective territory – but by a magical figure named Johnny Destiny, who appears one night from a motel swimming pool. Destiny is played by Tarantino, restlessly fidgeting his way through some fairly lame dialogue. (More than one critic has suggested he was too embarrassed to stand still and try to act.) It's believed he took the role to fulfil a promise made to the fellow director back at Sunset, and it has to be said that's certainly the way it plays.

Tarantino playing the part of Johnny Destiny – the name describes the character's true identity – in Jack Baran's Destiny Turns on the Radio.

Still, the parts kept on coming. In January 1995 he appeared in an episode of *All-American Girl*, the hit TV vehicle for stand-up comedienne/sometime Tarantino girlfriend, Margaret Cho. (It should be pointed out that 'girlfriend' is a word that should often be applied literally to Tarantino's case, as since his career got off the ground his girlfriends have sometimes enjoyed platonic best-buddy relationships. Sex seems at times to have been restricted to women who are admirers but not close friends.)

The episode was called 'Pulp Sitcom', and, as Tarantino explains, 'They hit damn near every touchstone from *Pulp Fiction* in the course of this episode, so it's pretty cool'. For once, the audience was probably having as much fun as the king geek himself was by appearing in it, as the show led up to a climax where one of Margaret Cho's television family is penetrated by a turkey skewer, à la Uma Thurman and the queasy hypo scene in *Pulp*. It demonstrates Tarantino's prominence in Hollywood that one of his movies should become so instantly recognisable that primetime TV can engage in a pastiche. More perversely, it also shows a young director who, after only two films, is happy and willing to engage in self-parody.

Tarantino with his friend Margaret Cho, on an episode of her TV show, All-American Girl, *entitled 'Pulp Sitcom'. Tarantino had great fun sending himself and his movie up – the type of self-parody old Hollywood directors never dared to attempt till their careers were washed up.*

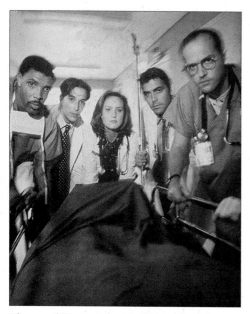

The cast of ER *converge around a casualty patient, in the episode directed by Tarantino. The directorial assignment – occurring during his 'year off' – was performed in return for videotaped episodes of the show. One patient has an ear severed in what appears to be a* Reservoir Dogs *reference, but Tarantino swears this was unintentional.*

Quentin's dalliance with TV – his first love, after all – wasn't confined to the Margaret Cho show. Late in 94, he contacted the producers of ER (emergency room), a medical drama originated by *Westworld/Jurassic Park* author Michael Crichton and produced by Steven Spielberg, to request tapes of episodes he'd missed while he was working. They were happy to oblige, on condition that he haul ass down to the set and direct an episode. Tarantino kept his side of the bargain – showing a characteristic former friends and associates from the Video Archives days are wont to deny exists, while fellow film-makers claim you can stake your life on his sticking to a promise. The script of that ER episode wasn't by Tarantino, but he was allocated the fastest-moving episode of the series on which to impose his performance-led shooting techniques and dramatic angles. There was, however, a scene with a female gang member who'd been admitted to the hospital with an ear missing.

The love affair with pop culture in general and TV in particular has led to rumours that Tarantino is about to direct an episode each of *Roseanne* and *Baywatch*. (At time of writing, it's not possible to verify.) These 'facts' might be products of the same rumour mill that insisted Tarantino would direct a movie based on the 60s TV spy series, *The Man From U.N.C.L.E.* which he himself has said, is a 'cool idea', but it's just not happening. For now, however, Tarantino is taking the smart step of ignoring any industry expectations and forming new creative partnerships within his own peer group.

Of the Sundance Institute generation – occasionally dubbed 'America's Nouvelle Vague', in tribute to the French New Wave of the late-50s that gave the film world Jean-Luc Godard – Allison Anders is perhaps Tarantino's closest buddy.

Another emigrant from the South, born in Ashland, Kentucky, almost ten years before Tarantino hit Knoxville, Anders spent a peripatetic younger life travelling all over the USA. Then from her late-20s to early 30s she studied film at UCLA – in contrast to Tarantino's own development. Her best-known film, *Gas Food Lodging* (1992 – it was her second, after *Border Radio* in 1986), which debuted at the Sundance Festival with *Dogs*, took a highly personalised tough/tender look at life for a single mother (like herself) and her daughters in Big Town USA.

Allison Anders' relationship with Tarantino was only stuck on the man-woman

Gas Food Lodging *(1992): Allison Anders' film was her second feature, and the first to gain widepread recognition.*

thing for a limited amount of time. As she says: 'You can't go out with other filmmakers. Kathryn Bigelow said, "Four times, no more." I go out on a date with Quentin, I've been editing all day, and he's telling me what's in his trim bin on *Dogs*.' The nascent romance may not have persisted, but the friendship certainly has.

Allison Anders followed *Gas Food Lodging* with *My Crazy Life*, a close-up on the members of an East LA Hispanic girls' gang. (Some of the characters were actually played by gang members, including one young girl called Nica who died from a drug overdose a few months after shooting concluded.) Before its completion, she had plans afoot for her next project, *Paul Is Dead*, based around the experiences and feelings of some teenage Americans at the time of the 'Paul McCartney is dead' rumours of the 1960s. She claims to have had a prior commitment from Hugh Grant to represent the British side of the story in the film, and was financed subject to his participation. Then, she says: 'Hugh dropped out for no reason.' With the still-birth of *Paul Is Dead*, the next full-length Anders project is *Grace of My Heart*, described as 'a singer-songwriter's journey through the 60s'. Before beginning that, however, she contributed to *Four Rooms*.

When called upon to opine on her friend's movies, she admits to a dislike of the violence, but stresses that any would-be imitators who define him by blood-soaked setpieces alone are missing a big part of the picture: 'What these guys don't understand is, you take the violence out of Quentin's movies, you've still got an incredibly exhilarating movie. You've got pop culture, fucking brilliant narrative structure, amazing composition. But with these other films [standard action/crime movies], you take the violence out and you don't have a movie.'

Tarantino himself was offering few clues as to where he would go from here. Despite misgivings about becoming the 'gun guy', he'd neither reject the visceral roughneck

Lawrence Bender

Tarantino's most long-term creative associate thus far, Lawrence Bender – now in his mid-30s – was producer on *Reservoir Dogs*, *Pulp Fiction* and *Four Rooms*. He began his career as a dancer, via a scholarship to *Fame* choreographer Louis Falco's dance academy. After suffering an injury which made dancing impossible, he studied acting with Sandra Seacat, who had previously tutored Jessica Lange and Mickey Rourke. After a short series of minor film and TV parts, he produced his first feature – Scott Spiegel's $125,000 psycho-thriller set during a supermarket night shift, *Intruder*. (An unexceptional but competent slasher thriller starring Sam Raimi, director of *The Evil Dead* and – more recently – *The Quick and the Dead*. Appropriately, the movie went quickly to video and died.)

An introduction to the struggling Tarantino proved the making of both of them, Bender being the pivotal figure who got *Dogs* off of the ground (see chapter 2). 'We could make *Reservoir Dogs* now for $15 million,' says Bender, 'but we wouldn't. We would make it for $3 million and make sure everyone got their money back. I have to balance business and the creative.'

Bender goes for a more hands-on approach than the traditional producer, however, the product being something more to him than just a magnet for investment: 'I'll be on the set and people will mistake me for the director, because Quentin will be saying, "We don't have the time and money for that shot,' and I'll be saying, "C'mon Quentin, I'll find the money for you. It's a great shot!"'

Bender claims the most important factors he – or any producer – can bring to a project are 'persistence, integrity and passion for the material'. In between *Dogs* and *Pulp*, he diversified by producing the debuts of two more new directors: Roger Avary's *Killing Zoe* and Boaz Yakin's *Fresh*, the latter a hardheaded, warmhearted piece of street life about a young black boy who runs errands for a drug dealer. Ever since *Dogs*' huge European success, Bender has found the market outside the USA to be fertile ground for his projects – slightly perversely, considering the difficulty in raising finance for a film in many of the countries concerned – with distributors prepared to put up part of the working budget if need be. 'I think that's one reason why foreign companies and people from Europe and Asia especially like what Roger and Quentin and Boaz do. It's because their movies have all these twists and turns, and that's where Europeans come from. It's a sudden revitalisation of a way of thinking.'

Ultimately, Bender relies on a simple maxim for working successfully with new or independent filmmakers: 'Don't sell out just to get something done.'

nature of his first movies, nor condemn outright the formularised product of the Hollywood machine.

'The most interesting thing is the story and the characters,' he has said of his own work. 'It exists on a completely human level. The thing that you get in our stuff is something that's otherwise lost in American cinema right now... I'm not one of these independent filmmaker guys that just bashes Hollywood, because I don't believe that – at the end of the year, there's usually at least ten really good, straightforward, no-apology Hollywood movies that come out of the studios. I think that's a pretty good average. So the system, while it could be better, still functions. Enough good work gets done by people who really care. But the thing that's really missing, from the overall output, and that really comes home when you look at films of the 70s, is that we have lost the art of telling a good story well. There is no storytelling going on right now in 85 percent of the movies that are made.'

Another of Tarantino's acting roles was in *Desperado*, Robert Rodriguez's first full-length feature since his remarkable Spanish-language gangster film *El Mariachi*, which was shot on an almost non-existent budget of $7000 and which he started while only 22. Originally planned as a big-budget remake for the English-speaking mass market, *Desperado* is now officially described as a sequel to a predecessor few of its intended audience will have seen.

Tarantino played the part of a minor character whose head is blown off his shoulders by gunfire. He had been Rodriguez's friend since *El Mariachi* previewed alongside *Reservoir Dogs* at the 1992 Sundance Festival. After *Desperado* Tarantino had plans for him (and, in the immediate future, for star Antonio Banderas). The first of those plans was called *Four Rooms*.

The much-anticipated *Four Rooms* is a compendium picture, subtitled by Tarantino in the script as *Four Friends Telling Four Stories Making One Film*. Although in some ways closer in conception to the *Dead of Night/Black Sabbath* prototype than *Pulp Fiction*, it doesn't adhere to any particular genre – though there's a basic comedy element linking the stories. With one segment written and directed by Tarantino, the basic structure of the film is given by linking sequences that star Tim Roth as a bellboy at LA's Chateau Marmont Hotel, and which are directed by Robert Rodriguez.

Four Rooms had its origin shortly after *Dogs* made its startling debut at 1992's Sundance Festival. Tarantino was initially approached by producer Doug Lindeman and his associates, who, as Tarantino implicitly acknowledges, wanted to group together five of the most exciting new directors in one project. 'We received a letter from them,' recalls Cathryn James, 'and Quentin signed an agreement.' The producers went into pre-production almost immediately, spending a sum estimated at up to $200,000. The universally strong reaction to his first feature, however, had brought about a change of plan for Tarantino. Instead of starting immediately on another project, he decided to spend most of the year on his tour of international film festivals

Tim Roth as the bellboy who links the four stories that make up Four Rooms.

promoting *Dogs*. 'I'll do it later, down the line,' he told his agent before hurriedly setting off.

A full two years further down the line, Tarantino decided to revive the project as *Four Rooms*, recruiting Robert Rodriguez, Allison Anders and Alexandre Rockwell, with the former taking a progressively more dominant role. His new representatives, the William Morris Agency (the most prominent group of agents in California), were forced to negotiate with an aggrieved Doug Lindeman when Cathryn James brought to their attention the documents she held relating to the original agreement. Ms James claims the original producers 'accepted a small compensation, and stepped away'.

By the time the group of directors came together on the project, the idea was embraced with enthusiasm and a spirit of cooperation. 'I thought that if there's this new-blood thing happening, it would be cool if we all did a film together,' says Rockwell, though he'd later find working alongside his more-famous friend to be a little more taxing that he may have first thought.

'It's amazing how well the four scripts worked together,' says Allison Anders, just as enthusiastic after the event. 'They were all black comedies. Mine was all women – a coven of witches trying to resurrect a goddess. Alex Rockwell's was a married couple having a serious problem in their marriage. Robert Rodriguez's was a family – mainly these little children who were left out on their own. Quentin's was a bunch of guys – party animals. The four parts were perfectly balanced. Pretty miraculous, really.'

Essentially, the movie appears to be the sum of four equal contributions, though Rodriguez embroiders a little more fabric around the edges. In practice, it seems that any factors which called for committee-style democracy were dominated by one person. 'When you work with Quentin, you can't try to rein him in,' says Alexandre Rockwell. 'It'd be like trying to talk a crack addict out of robbing you. Basically, you just listen to him talk for two hours.'

During the first group meeting, at the Chateau Marmont itself, much debate was expended on the name of the bellboy, the central linking character. 'The name was important in my story, and I didn't see it being so big in Quentin's story, but he wouldn't give,' says Rockwell, who wanted to christen the bellboy Benny. 'The thing is that 90 per cent of Quentin's ideas are great, and the 10 per cent that aren't great, he fights for just as hard.'

Wherein lies the secret of his success, perhaps. For his part, Tarantino – who wanted to call the Roth character Larry – claims, 'he doesn't look like a Benny; he isn't Benny. Somebody else might be Benny in some other movie that I do, but he wasn't Benny.'

'He had no use in my room except for his sperm [used for the witches' ritual],' deadpans Allison Anders, 'so I didn't care what his name was.'

The hair-splitting over the movie's minutiae reached such a level of intensity that Rodriguez decided to rig up his video camera to record events: 'You don't realize how much Quentin paces until you try and follow him with a camera. So I'd just let it sit and he would just pass in front of it once in a while.'

As the 10 November 1994 shooting date approached, Tarantino was able to give a quietly sardonic laugh about having left Anders and Rockwell to 'the lamest part of directing' – pre-production. 'Robert was off shooting [*Desperado*] and I had hit a fucking wall. I was doing 600 interviews on *Pulp Fiction* all around the world, so it was, like, "Guys, I'll see you on my week, alright? Just pretend it's a TV show and you guys are producing the show: you guys are Michael Mann and I'm Paul Michael Glaser."' (Director of *Miami Vice* / star of *Starsky and Hutch* respectively.)

Anders looked on her former boyfriend's renegade attitude with amused tolerance, comparing the working relationship to a family structure: 'Alex and I are the parents and Robert is the good son. Quentin is the bad son.'

Rockwell, slightly more resentfully, admits to feeling a little marginalised by his friend's brilliant career: 'The Quentin phenomenon is a little like making a film with Elvis Presley. There's a danger of this becoming Quentin and his friends, kind of like Spanky and his gang.'

Eventually, a minor crisis brought all four heads together on the same level. Steve Buscemi, for whom the bellboy part had been written, had decided it was too close to his bellhop role in the Coen Brothers' *Barton Fink*. He was asked to a meeting with the four filmmakers, only to hold to his guns. With all four recognising they were at an impasse, it was only a moment before Tarantino piped up and offered Buscemi a different part in his own 'room'. It was accepted.

'We were all sitting there rejected, and Quentin was only rejected for a second. I was more bummed out about that even than Steve passing,' recalls Anders. Recognising the others' nonplussed attitude and his own lack of tact, Tarantino genially withdrew the offer. 'It was that or else,' she laughs. The part went to Tim Roth, referred to enthusiastically by both Tarantino and Rockwell as the 'fifth auteur' for his contribution. And the bellboy's name is now Ted. (Other big names in the cast are Bruce Willis, Antonio Banderas and Madonna.)

In winter 1995/96, US moviegoers saw the result of Tarantino re-embracing his beloved horror genre. It remains to be seen whether Tarantino can make horror hip again, but then, if anyone can... The project itself is actually a Tarantino script – *From Dusk Till Dawn*, written almost simultaneously to *Reservoir Dogs* – directed by Robert Rodriguez. What makes it legitimately appear to be a Tarantino movie is, firstly, that Tarantino has delegated his script to a friend and favoured director, and secondly, and perhaps most relevant, is the continuing Tarantino/Rodriguez movie-making partnership, with its roots in *Four Rooms* and *Desperado*.

Back in 1990, Robert Kurtzman and John Esposito of special effects specialists KNB decided to make their own horror movie, rather than simply continuing to supply monsters and amputees to the industry. First, they needed a screenwriter who could work cheaply, and Kurtzman suggested an unknown writer whose first two scripts, *True Romance* and *Natural Born Killers*, had been shown to him by an agent. So out of this manic period of desperation and producitivity comes yet another project – Tarantino was actually preparing *Dogs* at the time, but was enticed away from his embryonic script by the princely fee of $1500 they were offering.

As Tarantino intimates, the situation was suggested by the would-be producers – he was paid to use one of his major talents, taking a situation and turning it into a story. At the Summer 1995 Weekend of Horrors, organised by *Fangoria* magazine in LA, guest of honour Quentin Tarantino told just what kind of a story his eager, youthful audience could expect:

'Seth and Richard Gecko [played by George Clooney, who Tarantino directed in *ER*, and the king geek himself] are bank robbers. Richard has just broken Seth out of a Texas prison, and because they're both cold-blooded killers, the entire state of Texas and the FBI want to lynch them. So they're making a mad dash for the Mexican border. In order to get across, they end up kidnapping a family on vacation in their motor home. They manage to sneak over the border and stop at a bar that happens to be run by vampires. The whole rest of the movie is us trying to fight the vampires off.'

Despite acting commitments from horror troupers such as Robert (Freddy Krueger, *Phantom of the Opera*) Englund, and Joseph Pilato – who appeared in *Day of the Dead* – all initial attempts to raise the budget failed. The script fell into the bottomless abyss of undeveloped projects, while Tarantino continued to develop his career. Five years on, and the glove was most definitely on the other fist. On the basis of his newfound fame, the screenwriter was able to resurrect the project with a $17 million budget, Rodriguez as director, and a cast including George Clooney, Juliette Lewis (from *Natural Born Killers*), Fred 'the Hammer' Williamson, splatter FX hero Tom Savini, and the Ubiquitous Brothers themselves, Harvey Keitel and Quentin Tarantino.

'This is not the typical vampire movie,' claims Rodriguez, explaining his enthusiasm for the project. 'This is just a strange breed of creature that has been in existence for centuries. There are things in this movie that are right out of left field. You won't even know when they're coming.'

Which sounds reassuringly in tune with Tarantino's playful attitude toward the crime genre. Tarantino himself echoed Rodriguez's sentiments: 'This is not going to be just another movie with actors with cheesey vampire teeth in their mouths. This is working in such a weird way that it sounds strange to even call them vampires. They're part vampire, part rat. They're just one sick bunch of monsters.'

Promisingly, Greg Nicotero of KNB, a horror genre stalwart, believes the revised version of the shooting script is the wildest project his company have worked on for years: 'I turned to page 70,' he laughs, 'and it said, "All hell breaks loose." I was sitting with Robert Rodriguez at the time and I asked him exactly what that meant. He said, "You wouldn't believe me if I told you, but..."'

So what of Tarantino's next personal directorial project? Wild guesses are as valid as rational deduction, with the ultimate film fan jumping like a grasshopper around so many genres. However, while it's still wide open, it's worth noting that Miramax – as well as setting up the Rolling Thunder distribution outlet, which allows the purchase of distribution rights for four films a year – have kept their boy wonder sweet by buying up the rights to four novels by Elmore Leonard. Tarantino is already back-pedalling on his 'goodbye to crime' statements, expressing a strong interest in directing one of the properties – *Killshot* – himself. If it comes off, it will be the first time he adapts a screenplay from a novel. And – given that Leonard is the acknowledged king of sharp-talking, wise-ass hoodlum dialogue – the first time he puts words in the mouths of characters created by a writer who's at least his equal. As to whose style will win out, or whether Tarantino's a big enough fan to try to assimilate Leonard's ouevre without taking it over – that's for the future, and it's all in the enjoyment of watching.

Filmography

Reservoir dogs

MR WHITE (Larry)   Harvey Keitel
MR ORANGE (Freddy)   Tim Roth
MR BLONDE (Vic)   Michael Madsen
NICE GUY EDDIE   Chris Penn
MR PINK   Steve Buscemi
JOE CABOT   Lawrence Tierney
HOLDAWAY   Randy Brooks
MARVIN NASH   Kirk Baltz
MR BLUE   Eddie Bunker
MR BROWN   Quentin Tarantino
TEDDY   Michael Sottile
SHOT COP   Robert Ruth
YOUNG COP   Lawrence Bender
SHOCKED WOMAN   Linda Kaye
SHOT WOMAN   Suzanne Celeste
THE VOICE OF K-BILLY, DJ   Steven Wright
Crew:
Casting by   Ronnie Yeskel
Music Supervisor   Karyn Rachtman
Radio Dialogue   Quentin Tarantino/Roger Avary
Costume Designer   Betsy Heimann
Special Make-up Effects   KNB EFX Group
Production Designer   David Wasco
Editor   Sally Menks
Director of Photography   Andrzej Sekula
Executive Producers   Richard N. Gladstein   Ronna B.
Wallace   Monte Hellman
Co-Producer   Harvey Keitel
Producer   Lawrence Bender
Written and Directed by   Quentin Tarantino
Music/Songs: Little Green Bag (J. G. Visser/
B. Bouwens), performed by George Baker Selection;
Stuck in the Middle with You (G. Rafferty/J. Egan),
Stealer's Wheel; I Gotcha, Joe Tex; Fool for Love,
Sandy Rogers; Hooked on a Feeling (M. James), Blue
Suede; Coconut, Harry Nilsson; Harvest Moon (J.
Joyce), Bedlam; Magic Carpet Ride (R. Moreve/J. Kay),
Bedlam; Wes Turned Country, Nikki Bernard; Country's
Cool, Peter Morris; It's Country, Henrik Nielson.

1992, 102 mins (Live America)

True romance

CLARENCE WORLEY   Christian Slater
ALABAMA WHITMAN   Patricia Arquette
CLIFFORD WORLEY   Dennis Hopper
MENTOR (Elvis)   Val Kilmer
DREXL SPIVEY   Gary Oldman
FLOYD   Brad Pitt
VINCENZO COCCOTTI   Christopher Walken
ELLIOT BLITZER   Bronson Pinchot
BIG DON   Samuel L. Jackson
DICK RITCHIE   Michael Rappaport

LEE DONOWITZ   Saul Rubinek
MARY LOUISE RAVENCROFT   Conchata Ferrell
VIRGIL   James Gandolfini
LUCY   Anna Thomson
NICKY DIMES   Chris Penn
CODY NICHOLSON   Tom Sizemore
Crew:
Casting by Risa Bramon Garcia / Billy Hopkins
Music Supervisor   Maureen Crowe
Costume Designer   Susan Becker
Special Effects   Robert Henderson / Larry Shorts
Prosthetic Make-Up Effects   Frank Carrisosa
Editors   Michael Tronick / Christian Wagner
Director of Photography   Jeffrey L. Kimball
Executive Producers   James G. Robinson Gary Barber
Bob Weinstein Harvey Weinstein Stanley Margolis
Co-Producers   Don Edmonds / James W. Skotchdopole
Producers   Bill Unger Steve Perry Samuel Hadida
Written by   Quentin Tarantino
Directed by   Tony Scott
Music: Hans Zimmer
Additional Music: Mark Mancina/John Van Tongeren
Songs: Graceland (Tonio K./C. Sexton), performed by
Charlie Sexton; In Dreams (J. Waite/M. Spiro), John
Waite; Wounded Bird (E. Chacon/C. Pettigrew/J.
Deutsch), Charles & Eddie; White Wedding, Billy Idol;
Skinny [They Can't Get Enough] (R. Bush), The Skinny
Boys; Heartbreak Hotel (M. Axton/T. Durden/E.
Presley), Val Kilmer; I Want Your Body (J. Ewbank/
M. Vander Kuy), Nymphomania; A Little Bitty Tear
 (H. Cochran), Burl Ives; I Need a Heart to Come Home
to (R. Smith/J. Jarvis), Shelby Lynne; Chantilly Lace
(J. P. Richardson), The Big Bopper; The Other Side
(S. Tyler/J. Vallance), Aerosmith; Raga Yaman, Clem
Alfor; (Love is) The Tender Trap (S. Cahn/J. Van
Heusen), Robert Palmer; Outshined (C. Cornell),
Soundgarden; All the Way (S. Cahn/J. Van Heusen) /
Learnin' the Blues (V. Silvers), Jerry Delmonico; Two
Hearts, Chris Isaak.

1993, 116 mins (Morgan Creek/Warner)

Pulp fiction

PUMPKIN   Tim Roth
HONEY BUNNY   Amanda Plummer
VINCENT VEGA   John Travolta
JULES WINNFIELD   Samuel L. Jackson
MIA WALLACE   Uma Thurman
BUTCH COOLIDGE   Bruce Willis
THE WOLF   Harvey Keitel
MARSELLUS WALLACE   Ving Rhames
LANCE   Eric Stoltz
JODY   Rosanna Arquette
FABIENNE   Maria de Madeiros

CAPTAIN KOONS   Christopher Walken
WAITRESS   Laura Lovelace
COFFEE SHOP   Roberth Ruth
MARVIN   Phil LaMarr
ROGER   Burt Steers
BRETT   Frank Whaley
FOURTH MAN   Alexis Arquette
PAUL   Paul Calderon
TRUDI   Bronagh Gallagher
BUDDY HOLLY   Steve Buscemi
BUTCH'S MOTHER   Brenda Hillhouse
KLONDIKE   Sy Sher
ESMARELDA VILLALOBOS   Angela Jones
DEAD FLOYD WILSON   Carl Allen
WILSON'S TRAINER   Don Blakely
PEDESTRIAN / BONNIE   Venessia Valentino
GAWKER   Karen Maruyama
HERSELF   Kathy Griffin
MAYNARD   Duane Whittaker
ZED   Peter Greene
THE GIMP   Stephen Hibbert
JIMMIE   Quentin Tarantino
MONSTER JOE   Dick Miller
RAQUEL   Julia Sweeney
YOUNG BUTCH   Chandler Lindauer
MARILYN MONROE   Susan Griffiths
MAMIE VAN DOREN   Lorelei Leslie
JERRY LEWIS   Brad Parker
DEAN MARTIN   Josef Pilate
JAMES DEAN   Eric Clark
ED SULLIVAN   Jerome Patrick Hoban
RICKY NELSON   Gary Shorelle
PHILLIP MORRIS PAGE   Michael Gilden
SHOT WOMAN   Linda Kaye
LONG HAIR YUPPIE SCUM   Lawrence Bender
HOLD HANDS YOU LOVE BIRDS"   Emil Sitka
SPORTSCASTERS   Robert Ruth Rich Turner
Crew:
Casting by Ronnie Yeskel / Gary M. Zuckerbrod
Music Supervisors Karyn Rachtman / Kathy Nelson
Costume Designer   Betsy Heimann
Special Effects   Wesley Mattox Stephen DeLollis Pat Domenico
Special Make-Up Effects   Kurtzman, Nicotero and Berger EFX Group
Editor   Sally Menke
Director of Photography   Andrzej Sekula
Executive Producers   Danny DeVito Michael Shamberg Stacey Sher Bob Weinstein Harvey Weinstein Richard N. Gladstein
Producer   Lawrence Bender
Stories by Quentin Tarantino / Roger Avary
Written and Directed by   Quentin Tarantino

Songs: Misirlou (F. Wise/M. Leeds/S. K. Russell/ N. Roubains), performed by Dick Dale & His Del-Tones; Strawberry Letter #23 (S. Otis), The Brothers Johnson; Bustin' Surfboards (G. Sanders/J. Sanders/ N. Sanders/L. Delaney), The Tornadoes; Son of a

Preacher Man (J. Hurley/R. Wilkins), Dusty Springfield; Lonesome Town (B. Knight), Ricky Nelson; Rumble / Ace of Spades (F. L. Wray, Sr./M. Cooper), Link Wray & His Raymen; Coffee Shop Music / Jungle Boogie (Ronald Bell/C. Smith/G. Brown/R. Mickens/ D. Boyce/R. Westfield/D. Thomas/Robert Bell), Kool & the Gang; Let's Stay Together (A. Green/A. Jackson, Jr./W. Mitchell), Al Green; Bullwinkle Part II (D. Rose/E. Furrow), The Centurions; Waitin' in School (J. Burnette/D. Burnette) – Gary Shorelle; Since I First Met You (H. B. Barnum), The Rodins; Teenagers in Love (W. Rosenauer), Woody Thorne; Girl You'll Be A Woman Soon (N. Diamond), Urge Overkill; Flowers on the Wall (L. Dewitt), The Statler Brothers; Comanche – The Revels; You Never Can Tell, Chuck Berry; If Love is a Red Dress (Hang Me in Rags), Maria McKee; Out of Limits (M. Gordon), The Marketts; Surf Rider (B. Bogle/N. Edwards/D. Wilson), The Lively Ones.

1994, 154 mins. (Morgan Creek/ Warner)

Natural born killers

MICKEY KNOX   Woody Harrelson
MALLORY KNOX   Juliette Lewis
WAYNE GALE   Roger Downey, Jnr.
DWIGHT McCLUSKEY   Tommy Lee Jones
MABEL   O-Lan Jones
PINBALL COWBOY   Ed White
SONNY   Richard Limeback
EARL   Lanny Flaherty
SHORT-ORDER COOK   Carol-Renee Modrall
MALLORY'S DAD   Rodney Dangerfield
MALLORY'S MOM   Edie McClurg
KEVIN   Sean Stone
WORK BOSSES   Jerry Gardner Jack Caffrey Leon Skyhorse Thomas
TV MALLORY   Corey Everson
DALE WRIGLEY   Dale Dye
GERALD NASH   Eddie "Doogie" Connor
DAVID   Evan Handler
ROGER   Kirk Baltz
JULIE   Terrylene
DEBORAH   Maria Pitillo
SOUNDMAN   Josh Richman
KIDS   Matthew Faber Jamie Herrold Jake Beecham
JAPANESE KIDS   Saemi Nakamura Seiko Yoshida
LONDON BOY   Jared Harris
LONDON GIRL   Katherine McQueen
FRENCH BOYS   Salvator Xuereb Emanuel Xuereb
FRENCH GIRL   Natalie Karp
YOUNG GIRL   Jessie Rutkowski
MICKEY'S MOM   Sally Jackson
MICKEY'S DAD   Phil Neilson
YOUNG MICKEY   Brian Barker
EMILY   Corinna Laszlo
GAS STATION ATTENDANT   Baltharzar Getty
JACK SCAGNETTI   Tom Sizemore
COWBOY SHERIFF   Red West

INDIAN COP   Gerry Runnels
YOUNG INDIAN BOY   Jeremian Bitsui
OLD INDIAN   Russell Means
PINKY   Lorraine Ferris
DRUGGIST   Glen Chin
JAPANESE REPORTER   Saemi Nakamura
KAVANAUGH   Puritt Taylor Vince
WURLITZER   Everett Quinton
DR. EMIL RHEINGOLD   Steven Wright
WGN NEWSCASTER   Robert Jordan
Crew:
Casting by Risa Bramon Garcia / Billy Hopkins /
Heidi Levitt
Casting Southwest: Sally Jackson
Casting Chicago: Jane Alderman
Music Producer   Trent Reznor
Costume Designer   Richard Hornung
Special Effects   Bob Stoker Larry L. Fuentes Steve
Luport Frank L. Pope Jim Schwalm Lucinda Strub
Visual Effects:
Supervisor   Rebecca Marie
Producer   Daniel Chuba
Animation: Colossal Pictures Animators / Wendy
Rogers / Cathy Wagner
Special Make-Up Effects   Matthew W. Mungle /
                                            Gordon J. Smith
Stunt Co-ordinator   Phil Neilson
Editors   Hank Corwin / Brian Berdan
Director of Photography   Robert Richardson
Executive Producers   Arnon Milchan Thom Mount
Co-Producer   Rand Vossler
Producers   Jane Hamser / Don Murphy/
                      Clayton Townsend
Story by   Quentin Tarantino
Written by   David Veloz / Richard Rotowski / Oliver
                      Stone
Directed by   Oliver Stone

Songs/Music Extracts: Waiting for the Miracle
(L. Cohen/S. Robinson) / Anthem / The Future, written
and performed by Leonard Cohen; Now, Chris
McGregor; The Way I Walk (J. Scott), Robert Gordon;
Noah Hutton Bug Spray – Otis Conner; Shitlist
(D. Sparks), L7; Control Room / Snakefield / Love to
Hánk / Shower / Wild Drone / Mallory Cello,
tomandandy; Moon Over Greene County – Dan Zanes;
La Vie en rose (M. David/E. Piaf/Louiguy), Victor Young
and his Singing Strings; Black Straitjacket – Elmer
Bernstein; Leader of the Pack (G. Morton/J. Barry/
E. Greenwich) – The Shangri-Las; The Trembler
(D. Eddy/R. Shankar) / Rebel-Rouser / Shazam!
(D. Eddy/L. Hazlewood), Duane Eddy; Rock & Roll
Nigger (P. Smith/L. Kaye), The Patti Smith Group; Me
and Her Outside – Steven Jesse Bernstein; Sweet Jane
(L. Reed) / If You Were the Woman and I Was the Man
(M. Timmins), The Cowboy Junkies; Wild Plate Rubs –
Scott Grusin; You Belong To Me (Pee Wee King/R.
Stewart/C. Price), Bob Dylan; Cartoonicide / B Swell,
Richard Gibbs; Kipenda Roho (R. Ongala), Remmy

Ongala & Orchestre Super Matimila; Back in Baby's
Arms (B. Montgomery), Patsy Cline; Taboo, Peter
Gabriel/Nusrat Fateh/Ali Khan; Ted Just Admit It,
Jane's Addiction; I Put a Spell on You (J. Hawkins) /
Judgement Day / Vena Cava (D. Galas) / The Lord is My
Shepherd (David), Diamanda Galas; History (Repeats
Itself) (T. Wilbrandt/K. Buhlert/F. Lovsky), A.O.S.;
Something I Can Never Have / A Warm Place
(T. Reznor), Nine Inch Nails; I Will Take You Home,
Russell Means; Drums-a-go-go (P. Buff), The Hollywood
Persuaders; On the Wrong Side of Relaxation / Under
Wraps / Checkpoint Charlie / The Violation of
Expectation, Barry Adamson; The Heat / In Doubt,
Peter Gabriel; Read My Lips (B. Lewis), Brent Lewis
and Richard Hardy; Earth, Peter Cater / R. Carlos
Nakai; These Boots Were Made For Walking (L.
Hazlewood) / Born Bad (C. Cobb), Juliette Lewis; The
Day the Niggaz Took Over (Dr. Dre/Snoop/Daz/Toni
C./RBX), Dr. Dre; Ghost Town (J. Dammers), The
Specials; The Hay Wain, Sergio Cervetti; The In Crowd
(B. Page), The Ramsey Lewis Trio; Doom Tac A Doom,
Brent Lewis; Spread Eagle Beagle (R. Osbourne),
Melvins; Cyclops, Marilyn Manson; Forkboy (J. Biafra/P.
Barker/A. Jourgensen/J. Ward/B. Rieflin), Lard;
Bombtrack / Take the Power Back (Z. de la Rocha /
Rage Against the Machine), Rage Against the Machine;
Fun (M. Elliott/M. Orleans/A. Noar/C. Negrete), Spore;
Allah, Mohammed, Char, Yaar (N. F. A. Khan), Nusrat
Fateh Ali Khan Qawwal and Party; Nusrat 1083/Nusrat,
Nusrat Fateh Ali Khan; Overlay (D. Bridie/J. Phillips/R.
McKinnon/R. Bradley/J. Southall/T. Cole), Not
Drowning, Waving; Sobama Moon (L. Eto), Kodo;
Wozzeck (A. Berg), The Paris National Opera Orchestra
and Chorus, Pierre Boulez, Walter Berry, Isabel
Strauss; Madame Butterfly (G. Puccini), The Sofia
National Opera Chorus and Orchestra; Carmina Burana
(C. Orff), The Prague Festival Orchestra and Chorus;
A Night on the Bare Mountain (M. Mussorgsky),
The Budapest Philharmonic Orchestra, J. Sandor.

1994, 119 mins. (Ixtlan/ New Regency/Warner)